Volume 14 of *Humanism Today*

Multiculturalism
Humanist Perspectives

edited by

Robert B. Tapp

in cooperation with the
North American Committee for Humanism

Prometheus Books

59 John Glenn Drive
Amherst, New York 14228-2197

Published 2000 by Prometheus Books

Inquiries should be addressed to
Prometheus Books
59 John Glenn Drive
Amherst, New York 14228–2197
VOICE: 716–691–0133, ext. 207
FAX: 716–564–2711
WWW.PROMETHEUSBOOKS.COM

04 03 02 01 00   5 4 3 2 1

ISSN 1058–5966
ISBN 9781573928052

For Information on Leadership Training and other programs, please contact:

THE HUMANIST INSTITUTE
2 West 64th Street
New York, NY 10023

CONTENTS

ACKNOWLEDGMENTS

Grateful acknowledgment goes to the authors for their willingness to revise their essays on a tight schedule. This editor has allowed some variations in ethnic labelings that may convey intended nuances. Thanks also to Paul Kurtz for facilitating the publication by Prometheus Books; to Editor-in-Chief Steven L. Mitchell for his wise suggestions; and to my wife, Ana Martinez, proofreader and pillar.

Earlier volumes of *Humanism Today* have been published by The Humanist Institute, which was founded in 1982 by the North American Committee for Humanism (NACH) as an educational venture to train professional and lay leaders for existing humanist organizations. The guiding principle has been that studying together would enhance all forms of nontheistic humanism, whether they described themselves as religious or secular; Ethical Culturist, Unitarian Universalist, Humanistic Jew; rationalist; freethinker.

More than eighty students have completed a three-year graduate level curriculum. The Institute's adjunct faculty has gathered annually to consider pressing topics, and these chapters grow out of the 1999 colloquium. The adjunct faculty will be reassembling in 2000 to consider Eco-humanism.

Robert B. Tapp

PREFACE

Few of the contemporary culture wars are as hotly contested as the battle over 'multiculturalism.' The battlefields are dispersed—school boards, town councils, state legislatures, universities, urban planners, journalists, politicians, political pundits, talk-show hosts. The ambiguities are even more glaring. Is the demand simply to give greater recognition to an existing pluralism? Or to preserve cultures by withdrawals and self-segregations? Or to shape a new identity from presently separated ones (*E pluribus unum*)?

What do we mean by 'culture'? Should we be listening to the anthropologists or the historians, the politicians or the pollsters? Where should we position bicultural and polycultural persons? 'Hybridization' has become a hot topic among sociologists and anthropologists, along with 'diaspora'. Given the rising percentages of ethnic intermarrying, this is the future. And the displaced emigrants very often transform the old home cultures whether they ever return or not.

We need to remember that cultures have time-dimensions as well as space-dimensions. Somali culture, for instance, is very different in East Africa, in Kenya refugee camps, and in U.S. cities.

Add to this heady brew the impact of globalization, and the confusion almost overwhelms. Globalization, however, is the solvent of time and place. V. S. Naipaul observed that he felt closer to his friends around the world, regardless of color, creed, or nationality than he felt toward his own grandparents.

> This idea of the pursuit of happiness is at the heart of the attractiveness of the civilization of modernity to so many outside it or on its periphery. I find it marvelous to contemplate to what an extent, after two centuries, and after the terrible history of the earlier part of this century, the idea has come to a kind of fruition. It is an elastic idea; it fits all men. It implies a certain kind of society, a certain kind of awakened spirit. I don't imagine my father's Hindu parents would have been able to understand the idea. So much is contained in it: the idea of the individual, responsibility, choice, the life of the intellect, the idea of vocation and perfectibility and achievement. It is an immense human idea. It cannot be reduced to a fixed system. It cannot generate fanaticism. But it is known to exist, and because of that, other more rigid systems in the end blow away. [1]

Such comments remind us that some of the older markers of difference—skin pigmentation, hair texture, facial features, manners—lose valence in a world committed to an expansion of human rights—where we have learned to attend to disabilities and discriminations based on gender, sexual orientation, juvenile status, mental and physical ability.

This new set of problems/values, emerging in the industrialized world but spilling over into almost every remote corner of the planet, changes many rules of the game. Chivalry, as an example, becomes sexism; 'civilizing activities,' whether of Belgians in the former Congo or British in India or Yankees in the Philippines are now more accurately seen as imperialism and paternalism.

The chapters in this book grow out of the 1999 annual meeting of the adjunct faculty of The Humanist Institute.[2] Members gathered for two days in April to critique each other's drafts. Previously, these annual conferences have been published in the journal *Humanism Today,* and the present volume constitutes number 14 in that series. The Institute founded in 1982 to keep in dialogue otherwise contentious humanists, also trains humanist leaders and spokespersons in a three-year course of study. The Institute from its beginnings has been committed to a naturalistic and nontheistic humanism.

This form of humanism look back to Greco-Roman, Renaissance, and Enlightenment predecessors. Modern science is seen as the best embodiment of human intelligence. While an evolutionary universe has no "purposes" of its own, and we have no evidence of powers outside of our universe, intelligence permits (and demands) a reconstruction of the universe better to serve and expand human values. Most religions, with their imaginary cosmic helpers and putatively alternative worlds which promise escape, belittle human powers and possibilities. Current millennial fevers, for instance, anticipate some kind of divine intervention that will accomplish what we humans are unable to do. Consider, for example, the Biblical tower of Babel as a mythical condemnation that sees human effort as futile arrogance.

Religions in their better moments have claimed to supply knowledge and wisdom that goes beyond anything that we can attain. At their worst, they have condemned our efforts as sinful pride and demanded that we accept the status quo as divinely decreed.

Many readers have found this situation epitomized in Albert Camus' novel *The Plague*. When the disease strikes the North African city, Fr. Paneloux implores citizens to examine their lives in order to discover why they have brought such divine punishment upon themselves. Doctor Rieu, the humanist physician, instead begins an unceasing labor to find a vaccine. Paneloux's sermon after a year of the plague is somewhat more reticent, suggesting that such tribulations are part of God's mystery. When the disease strikes him, his piety submits to it and rejects medical help. Rieu persists in his research, unable to believe in a God who "kills small children." A third character [Camus' alter ego?] says that he "once wanted to be a saint, but now knows that it is even more difficult to become a man."

The novel can of course be read as a parable against Nazism. But in any reading it spells out the uncertainty and challenge of living in a problematic universe that is lacking any comforting patterns.

The final editing of this volume has been interspersed with five weeks of travels in Western Europe, underscoring some of the differences between U.S. multiculturalism and the present European situations. Consider our own history. Start with the colonizing by Spanish, British, French, Dutch, and Russians—outsiders who (with the partial exception of Penn's fellow Quakers) genocidally decimated the Native American population. There followed a massive importation of African slaves. Humanist readings of the new republic have viewed Washington/Jefferson/Franklin/Madison as architects of "the Enlightenment-made-flesh," and have seen the Civil War and Lincoln as not only ending the abomination of slavery but spreading those ideals to the whole of society and not just the central federal government. Sidney Mead, distinguished historian, views Lincoln as America's "greatest theologian."[3] In the ensuing industrialization, the new country profited from Europe's political, economic, and religious woes, attracting waves of immigrants eager to shed much of their pasts. Emerson had already described his America as a "smelting pot." Under WASP hegemony, immigrant Jews and Catholics liberalized doctrinally as they Americanized. The absence of an official national religion has always tempered U.S. anticlericalism, and has at the same time created a spawning ground for variant denominations and new religions. One could well argue that this proliferation of religiosities was the earliest proof of the power of free markets!

However the power and persistence of fundamentalism in the United States suggests another metaphor from the economists. Gresham's law predicts that bad money will always drive out good. Many argue that fundamentalism reflects a fear of change, a fear of choice (which is what change demands). I take fundamentalism to be an unswerving commitment to some past event claimed to be both historical and understandable. The giving of one text by some divine process of revelation/dictation—Torah, New Testament, Koran, Nichiren, *Book of Mormon*, *Science and Health*, *Isis Unveiled*, Casteñeda's Don Juan. Viewed from this perspective, fundamentalists are those who can abide neither pluralism nor change. And the U.S. population is presently about 40 percent fundamentalist—people who want Darwin and the Big Bang to fade away and Scriptural sufficiencies to survive and to satisfy. The rest of us, that underwhelming majority, presumably want science to continue, somehow, as seedbed of the technology that the whole world cherishes. Any theoretical exploration of multiculturalism must, for the United States, come from this 60 percent who actually live in the modern world. The fundamentalists will have only condemnation for anything less than a monoculture on their terms. In other words, the political dimension of multiculturalism, which must include the fundamentalists, is very different from the intellectual analysis from which they have excluded themselves.

From a European perspective, where fundamentalism is much rarer, the U.S. situation appears bewildering. U.S. shock over presidential philandering seems an out-of-date Puritanism. And our debate over evolution ('it's just a theory!') seems ludicrous. After all, the Vatican (hardly noted for progressivism) endorsed evolution (with the proviso that the "human soul" must be affirmed as "specially created"). The contrasts remain, however. "Ethnic cleansing" in the former Yugoslav Republic flourished for too long before concerted reaction from the rest of Europe. The French delegate insists that an emerging European Union must leave French culture undiminished. Margaret Thatcher was cheered when she told her Conservative Party that the United Kingdom was "the best" in Europe, and that all bad things had come from the Continent. Germans debate whether immigrants can become citizens, and an anti-immigrant party scores at the Austrian ballot box. *Le Figaro* headlines a story "Multiethnic France?" Russia, arguably not part of Europe, has never recovered from the Lenin/Stalin solution of "autonomous ethnic republics" for all non-Slavs, and successive Moscow governments show little will to incorporate Islamic or Asian cultures into a retrenched Mother Russia.

Which brings us back to the United States as the place where multiculturalism has been most theorized and most explored. At one extreme are the Glazer's and Schlesinger's, decrying the polarization and holding out little hope of resolution. Martin Marty in a recent book gravitates toward "sentiment and affection" as being attainable sinews to hold together the antagonists until they can understand and appreciate each other's stories.[4] However laudable this aim, it founders on the issue of fact. What if the story (theirs or ours, it doesn't matter) is discovered to be untrue or, at the very least, unlikely? We are thrown back to the bedrock issue of criteria, of credibility. And unless we are steeped in postmodernism, this is a central issue.

For more than a century, scholars have probed the permutations of our myths. Those in the tradition of Mircea Eliade contend that any story beginning "Once upon a time..." is mythical, and thus not subject to historical or critical scrutiny as to its temporal accuracy. But what do we do with those stories that are allegedly historical accounts. "U.S. ships were attacked in the Tonkin gulf...." What was once taken by many to be history now turns out to be story, and we surely must accept that there are many ways to make such a distinction between story and history. While we can never fully reconstruct (in today's jargon "represent") any past event, we inevitably scrutinize accounts comparatively, interview observers, examine records, and ultimately poll the jury of responsible scholars.

Of equal importance is what humans do with their rescrutinized stories and histories. The slave trade that plagued the Americas into the nineteenth century affords a good example. The stories about how this practice was once viewed by many as normal and then came to be seen as sinful/immoral/illegal/unprofitable have been quite carefully winnowed into "histories" by generations of scholarly debates. While slavery persists in many parts of the world, these histories serve both to make render it visible and to highlight its human costs. The issues for most of us would be to keep these histories alive in human consciousness in a "Never again!" manner and to probe our psyches and cultures and civilizations for those most most difficult "What now!" responses. Should we hesitate in moving toward a better society, using "Because of..." as an excuse? Or do we move on saying "Despite..."

Put this in terms of Richard's Dawkin's felicitous term "meme" for those persistent/replicating ideas within cultures. Just as the gene can be either expressed or suppressed, so can the meme. Julian Huxley long ago argued that once we understood the mechanisms of evolution we became responsible for it. This is even truer for social evolution. Education is the great change agent, and it is driven by the imaginations of humans. Do they settle for adjusting to their worlds, or do they work to transform those worlds. The answer will hinge on which stories they choose to cherish—and which to correct. What is true for modern humans is that the stories are in a continual process of being shared and critiqued. The outcome is the transformation into history, the thing John Dewey called "warranted assertabilities."

An instructive exercise for U.S. readers might be to peruse a new Dutch publication, *Representing the Japanese Occupation of Indonesia.* The editor begins by noting that:

> Three countries were involved in the Japanese occupation of the Indonesian archipelago [1941-45], three countries which each experienced and interpreted the war in its own way. In each of them the memories of the occupation have been embedded in the history of the nation. This is characteristic of every history of war and violence: a country remembers its own dead, and interprets the suffering in the same national terms in which the war was waged or experienced. The memory is determined to a large extent by self-justification and an emphasis by each country on its own role as victim.[5]

Today's reader will note one major omission here. The fourth country was Portugal with its colony in Timor until 1975! But the book graphically reminds us that the nation-building commitment of European colonization inevitably generated a resistant local nationalism. In this case that nationalism was fostered and used by the Japanese during their military occupation. How determine whether they were primarily liberators or oppressors? How should/did Indonesians regard them after their own independence in 1949. How did each of these parties relate to subsequent regimes in each other's countries. This fascinating volume continually brings its modern readers up short with testimonies of the participants, photographs from that distant time and place, and counter-interpretations of "what happened."

This painful sorting and re-interpreting of past memories is the very essence of moving from stories to history [only ideally as a singular account]. An Italian city hall lists those local citizens who died for their country 1939-45 [but this means some died fighting with the Nazis and some fighting against them]. As the crimes of Stalin and his allies come into clearer focus, the significance of World War II "resistance fighters" in France becomes more prob-lematic.[6] As U.S. scholars from the 1960s write the histories of the 1960s, all the tensions between a "new left" and an "old left" resur-face. *Sic transit gloria mundi*!

Not only are the stories that cultures carry subject to this kind of critique, so are their myths—those Ur-stories that have proved so enduring. Can cultures cling to creationism (an erstwhile Biblical derivation, still embraced by fundamentalists) or the Shinto myth of creation by the stirring of the sea or the Hindu myths of the sleep of Vishnu or the drum-shaking of Siva? In the future museum of the humanist, these will all be exhibited as creative fictions that once served human needs now long-outgrown. Alongside those ex-hibits will be many more illustrating the visions and values that have emerged among us since the rise of modern science. Utopian-isms, Deisms,[7] romanticizations of nature,[8] free thinkers,[9] democ-racy and human rights pioneers. Elsewhere in that museum (maybe in its right wing) will be exhibits of monarchists, emperors, left and right totalitarian dictators, military juntas, nationalists, chauvinists, racists, sexists, homophobes, child abusers, nihilists, and fanatics of exclusive religions.

Notes

1. "Our Universal Civilization," *New York Times,* November 5, 1990. Excerpt from Walter B. Wriston lecture at the Manhattan Institute.

2. The Institute is one of the principal activities of the North American Committee for Humanism (NACH) which was founded in 1982. The website is:

   http://www.humanism.net/institute/

3. *The Nation with the Soul of a Church* (New York: Harpers, 1975).

4. Martin E. Marty, *The One and the Many* (Cambridge: Harvard University Press, 1997).

5. Remco Raben, ed. (Zwolle: Waanders Publishers for Netherlands Institute for War Documentation, 1999), p. 7.

6. Stéphane Courtois and others, eds., *The Black Book of Communism: Crimes, Terror, Repression* (Cambridge: Harvard University Press, 1999).

7. Thomas Paine, Thomas Jefferson, James Madison, and their many predecessors.

8. M. H. Abrams classic *Natural Supernaturalism: Tradition and Revolution in Romantic Literature.*(New York: Norton, 1971) deserves a regular rereading.

9. Robert Ingersoll, Mark Twain, Bertrand Russell come to mind as both philosophically sophisticated and communicatively eloquent.

1

BORDER SKIRMISHES AND MULTICULTURALISM

NOTES FROM THE FIELD

Harvey Sarles

Political correctness! It's our culture and we can do what we want and need to...do! Old white guys! Late capitalism and the hegemony of the West! You can't understand us unless you're one of us! Deconstruct this! Modernism, rationality, progress, and the enlightenment: past and passe! Great Books! A Common Culture and Cultural Literacy! Bah! It's all over! The Culture Wars! This is a postmodernist era!

Cliches and diatribes which wax and wane in the hallowed halls of universities and sometimes in the (sur)real world. Much of the battle occurs in the academy among those who locate themselves in the Humanities and Literature. But they also characterize the arguments made by some powerful nations who oppose the ideas of International Human Rights as Western rationalism sticking its noses into others' businesses. *Human nature: Bah! Culture: Yes!*

Much of the current discussion about multiculturalism entails a set of polemics which might be described as *border skirmishes*: some arguments or positions which lay claim to socio-political or intellectual turf, directed against other positions which also have some currency. They operate as dialectics for some thing or some groupings of persons and against (often implicitly) some other dominant or convenient ideas. Border skirmishes, that is, always seem to include politics—somebody and/or some ideas gaining while their opponents lose—while the grounds of their arguments often include intellectual issues.

Recent attacks against, and alternatives to reason, include a range of issues which purport to be for *culture* and oppose whatever are its opposites; usually *nature*. In some contexts these seem to be attacks on science. In others, issues often involve questions of politics and justice; e.g., whether the concept or idea of *nature* is somehow used to favor one group of people over others, an old but resilient idea which resurfaces in this era of genetic engineering and determinism.

In the academy some of these border wars include attacks on reason and on the establishments of science. The "Two-Culture Problem" of the Sciences vs. the Humanities first pointed out by C. P. Snow in the late 1950's has not abated.[1] The religious attack on science focuses primarily—but not totally—on evolution. In common, they are polemics about the location of the texts of life: what I consider the World-as-Text vs. the Text-as-World. They include questions of truth and method; but particularly of the nature and location of authority.

While it often seems easy to choose one side or the other over any particular pique, the contexts and histories of these attacks or arguments are worth exploring to see what they may carry inside their modern or postmodern baggage.

In order to give them some deserved depth it is useful to fill in some background against which the current tides of multicultural movements and moves can be given some flesh.

But first, what are some examples of border skirmishes, who are the parties, and what shapes do these polemics take?

A. The attempt to develop and defend multicultural curricula, ethnic schools, and Black Language movements: separatism in various guises. NAACP lawsuit in Minneapolis over redeveloping community (often segregated) schools vs. integrating city and suburban students—in both directions. Required courses in Cultural Pluralism at the University of Minnesota. Is our democracy color-blind?

B. The battle between young(er) women and older men over who gets to teach in higher education; and the feminist movement as a more general protest against the hegemony of white males. Neo-conservatives vs. the politically correct (neo)neo-Marxists and Cultural Studies faculties as it is now playing-out in the universities.

C. Great Books and Political Correctness: a battle in the Humanities over the control of culture, knowledge, and curriculum. Do we read (and believe) that the Great Ideas were almost all written by white European men who died a long time ago? Or do we acknowledge women and people of color as thinkers in the ongoing, in these times? More widely, it represents a splintering of American politics into various forms of new conservatism vs. progressivism (vs. neither-of-the-above).

D. Science vs. the Humanities (and Fundamentalist Religion). Do the ideas of the enlightenment—reason and rationality and the general sense of progress of modernism—still hold, or is this a post-modern era? Questions of truth, authority, the status and politics of humans. Who is smarter: men/women, white/others? Who gets into science? Are we moving from democracy to theocracy? Whose words are better?

E. Claims of some countries that their nation or culture is different from others, and that they have the right to determine how to treat their people: e.g., China and questions of human rights abuses.

Multiculturalism

From the moment in the 1954 Supreme Court decision, Brown vs. the Board of Education, there has been a growing sense that Jim Crow laws still prevail at some level of law and thinking in this country: first legal slavery until 1865, then Jim Crow in 1896, now the jailing of so many young African-American males on counts of drugs and gangs; most recently, racial profiling in police deciding who to detain on suspicion.

In these contexts, multiculturalism is a cover term for the attempt to organize or conceptualize a Black (and/or other) community under the rubric of a distinct culture: separate schools, curricula, holidays, histories, self-esteem—resulting from the idea that the Black commmunity is conceptualized as something other—but especially as lesser—by the majority population.

Culture becomes a conceptual tool for legitimization and a sense of equality against a larger white community which still feels hostile, especially in its representative police, and in the fact that public education continues to serve the African-American community less well than majority communities or cultures. Here, *culture* becomes an apologetic or rallying cry for difference, independence, and legitimization against the sense of homogenization that the majority claims and apparently believes.

It is an attempt to own (to co-opt) the term *culture* to justify the fact of any particular grouping of persons who have a common history or outlook. It is used, often, by those whose identity is set—at least in great part—by others, as a mode of taking control of their destiny. Black History, and Black/African-American schools and studies are attempts to own an identity by which others discriminate. Examples include the writing of Afro-American curricula in some states (New York), the development of Afrocentric schools and academies, issues of the use of *Black Language*.[2]

More clear, perhaps, has been the attempt by a group (*Act Up*) of gay (mostly lesbians) persons to own the term *Queer*, as a way of gaining pride in a (formerly) derogative term, rather than reacting weakly or remaining hidden as they were accused of being...*Queer*.

The Modern Concept of Culture

The modern concept of culture—as well as books and the United Nations Universal Declaration of Human Rights—stem from the work of Franz Boas, his students, and colleagues, notably John Dewey. Boas established cultural anthropology in America and was teacher to Ruth Benedict, Margaret Mead, and Ashley Montagu among many others at Columbia University. Montagu and Pedro Comas were Boas' students who drafted the Universal Human Rights Declaration. According to Alan Ryan's recent biography, Boas was probably the strongest influence on Dewey during his years at Columbia. Thus culture has moved through educational and philosophical thinking.

This is to say that the concept of culture and the idea of universality of aspects of the human condition have not always been at odds, as they seem to be in this moment of multiculturalism. But more about this later.

Boas' work takes place principally during the time of the mass European immigrations to America before and after the turn of the 20th century. He attempted to wed three sometimes distinct approaches to the definition of the human into one discipline: culture, language, and the physical, all to be Anthropology. His approach to Anthropology was dominant in the field until the 1950s when British Social Anthropology became more popular, and linguistics and physical anthropology either drifted away or were relegated to lesser status.

Boas had two major tasks: a) the attempt to bring all peoples of the world into the human family; b) attempt to alleviate various forms of racism and discrimination in America directed particularly toward European immigrants: Catholic and Jewish primarily, but including other recent immigrants.

a) Until well into this century, many of the peoples of/from the thirrd world—including Indigenous/American Indians—were considered *inferior* by their nature. Terms such as *barbarians* and *savages* were not infrequent in describing native peoples. Boas' students went to many parts of the world and lived doing fieldwork with the native peoples, described and wrote their languages, described and compared their cultures and physical relations and differences. Boas, himself, wrote essays on how facial appearance changes in immigrant populations over a few generations to look like—in this case—other Americans.[3]

Gradually, most American have come to accept the idea that the world's peoples are of a single kind: human; and that they do not represent various levels of human development. In this case, culture was the concept utilized to show that the differences among peoples are small and explicable, and not due to some populations or languages being *civilized*, while others remain somehow at the level of lesser species. (The term *civilization* will arise later as the site of some current border skirmishes, especially in the academy.) I think that Boas' accomplishments in this arena were astounding, particularly when we become aware of the historical situation concerning the nature-culture of the peoples of the world.[4]

But he also promoted ideas which have been adopted/co-opted in various contexts of relativism: every culture/person is human and equal to all others at least in terms of rights and life chances. As it was opposed to ideas of nature as being determinate or fixed, it fought various forms of racism within the idea of culture as changeable. These polemics still wander in the mazes of multiculturalism, and seem to be being resuscitated in various contexts even (perhaps especially) within the academy.[5]

Perhaps the most anti-Boasian current movement is the use of culture to claim separateness and the idea that one must be a member of a particular culture to be able to understand what it means to be, say, Chinese or Afro-American (or a woman). Thus it turns out to be a polemic about knowledge, privilege, power: who gets to determine the nature of the future, of education, and so on. Here, many of the former ideas of the fixity and predetermination of nature have been transduced to its former opposition of *culture*. One senses that this is deeply ironic.[6]

b) The situation in America around the turn of the twentieth century was akin to the present: huge immigrations from parts of Europe especially Eastern and Southern Slavic and Italian Catholic communities, and an important (because it riled the ruling WASPs) Jewish presence in East Coast cities, which began about 1883 after the start of the Russian pogroms with the ascension of Tzar Nicholas II in 1881. There were about the same percentage of non-native English speakers here when Reed-Nelson anti-immigration bill was enacted in 1924.

Much of Boas' work attempted to show that the immigrants were not much different from the older European populations in America; that given three generations or so they would look and sound much alike. His work was very successful in the long run: particularly as it has resonated since the end of WWII: consider the idea of Jewish Michael Douglas playing the President of the United States in a recent movie—without any public comment. But in 1924, the very angry anti-immigration bill was drafted so that immigration numbers reverted to whatever the percentage of population was in America prior to 1880, halting Slavic, Italian, perhaps particularly Jews from further immigration until 1965.

Will we pass another anti-immigration bill in the near future, this time focused particularly on Hispanics and Asians, taking us back to the times when Boas developed and elaborated the democratic ideals of equality among all of humankind? Here multiculturalism signals the rising of this very old battle for who and what is America and American.

Literature and Liberal Humanism

Liberal humanism is a term and idea which emerged in England during the middle of the nineteenth century, when the attempt to teach literature over religion made its first mark in British universities. Higher education in Britain until that period, and even later in America, was primarily to educate the wealthy and the future leaders of churches. Only after Darwin, in America in the 1860's, were there attempts to teach science and the Liberal Arts in the universities of America. Liberal Humanism was/is a polemic against the idea of religion determining the human condition and our life directions.

Questions of authority arose—a continuing theme in the border battles in multiculturalism etcetera—at first to battle powerful religious claims to truth. In literature, Matthew Arnold, particularly, attempted to establish the idea that certain literatures and particular authors had sufficient genius or quality of thinking and writing to establish them as legitimate inspirers of each present moment: the

Great Books and all that flowed from this movement in the hands especially of Mortimer Adler in America.[7] In these contexts, culture referred less to Boas' ideas of change, and more to the idea of a cultivated or civilized mind being the direction of a good education: high culture.[8] Ideas of social and political privilege also permeated the Great Books movement.

As America has moved into the current Culture Wars since the 1960s, neo-Conservatives in the Humanities have taken the path of High Culture/Civilization opposed to the politically correct ideas derived from (neo)Marxism and the various writers who have gathered under the rubrics of Critical Theory, deconstructionism, and postmodernism.[9]

In its zeal to take apart the foundations of Western thought, the return to the hegemony of the text and narrative—an attempt to fight off the notion of the representatives of high culture and to return power to (all) the people—narrativity has not only fought the Great Books, high culture and civilization movements, but it has also engaged science, free inquiry, and any notions of rationality which have underlain a great deal of the Humanist thinking.[10]

In this moment of virtual reality, changes in the nature of communication via e-mail, changes in the nature of writing which accompany these changes, many of our students find these changes very inviting and comfortable.

Lastly in this context, the rise of narrativity in the contexts of postmodernism and various attacks on enlightenment rationality, shares with religious fundamentalism the notion that the subject—even any notions of reality—lies within texts. Interpretation or exegesis become the central subject matter of our very being. The stage is set increasingly for a return to religion. And as all of this entails politics, the possibility of a move from (promise, at least, of) democracy to theocracy raises the importance of the stakes from academic infighting to the Realpolitik.

Postmodernism

The longer-larger goal of the postmodernism movement—most *literary criticism/theory*—is to undo Western thought from Plato to the present: *destruct*, Heidegger's more ambitious project, and Derrida's *deconstruct*—to attempt to take apart the edifice brick-by-brick. What it might be toward—remains less clear—especially since the fall of the Soviet Union, and the sense that Marxism-communism no longer represents any contrary to Western thought. Its goal thus remains less than clear. Its current strategy is to re-think itself...for the foreseeable future.[11]

The attempt is to co-opt the ideas of knowledge and truth by replacing—better, including—science and all it entails, as aspects of narrativity: science tells stories...just like everyone else. The question, just as in the religious *scientific creationist* attack on *scientific evolutionism*, comes down to which (if any) are the valid and authoritative stories.

The primary locus of this polemic has to do with how we arrive at reality: the World-as-*Text* of science and rationalism assumes or takes the *natural world* to be the locus of its studies. Humans are not always included in this mode or locus of knowledge study—part of the complaint of the other side(s). Humans as observers, objective or remote from their observations, seem often self-serving, and usually enmeshed in some form of politics, whether they admit it or not.

The other side, postmodernists (but also religious fundamentalists) begin from a deep sense that there is a textual-historical foundation to all of knowing. All of science turns out, like other texts, to be forms of narrative, of tellings. Questions of observation, experimentation, etc. turn out in their telling to be forms of understanding what their colleagues are telling about the world.[12]

On a few issues, I find myself being somewhat sympathetic with the postmodernists: 1) that there is some politics to most scientific endeavors—especially when it has to do with the human condition. Science and technology have been primarily white guys' games;[13] 2) there is much to the story of texts and history. And it is not just the postmodernists who play these games, but a good deal of behavioral biology and psychology; 3) current claims about the innateness of language and the brain and evolution are rife with Platonic panoramas. These claims are easily continuous with the history of racist thought, and lend themselves to a resurgence of eugenics.

My understanding of the human nature issues as played out in most sociobiology, is that it is loaded with Aristotelian presumptions: e.g., the uniqueness of human language and mind due to the symbolic nature of our language.[14] My sardonic comment is that if it repeated often enough, its truth becomes obvious and presumptive. Parallel to this, is the current reading of the interactions of other species: we are very quick to judgment from behavior to politics (Alpha males and all that!). Somehow, if it is stated in the name of Science it has a different (and more acceptable status) than other textual claims to truth.[15]

I suggest that we need to probe claims to truth: how do textual truths get understood: interpretation (exegesis, in the religious textual contexts) and arguments about authority are played with quite extensively by postmodernists, whose lines of attack are often to undermine any and all claims to authority (even their own), leaving us gasping in the nothingness of nihilism.[16]

But merely to oppose postmodernism and merely to defend modernism, is to take them and ourselves less seriously than we all deserve. Here we continue to talk past one another, and avoid the tough critical analysis of all positions...which we humanists claim as our strength. It is too easy to dismiss opposing ideas by looking only at what we disagree with, and not examining the broader contexts of our own predilections. As Whitehead taught us, most modern thinking is footnotes to Plato, where the experience of our sensory being is captivated by the shadows in Plato's cave, urging us to deal not with our being, but with stories of our being.

Modernism? It might not hurt to read a bit of the American pragmatists from Charles Sanders Peirce to John Dewey and George Herbert Mead, and see what our experience has to do with our thinking.

The End of Rationalism

The University in Ruins. Bill Readings wrote this book shortly before he died in a plane crash over northern Indiana.[17] His point, following Kant and the idea of the German University, is that rationalism is tied intimately with the idea of the (rational) state. The real issue is that the idea of the state is changing rapidly, and the university follows and/or represents the idea of the state: globalism, technology, multinationals, etc. There is thus no particular issue of postmodernism or of any pervasive multiculturalism. Only that the nature of the nation-state is moving beyond any sense of being which would have sustained a sense of the rational. There is only the question of the world, the globe, and where oh where can we find any meaning to rationality, to the university, to...? Border skirmishes? Bah!

Notes

1. C. P. Snow, *The Two Cultures and the Scientific Revolution.* (New York: Cambridge University Press, 1959)

2. The history of the notion of Black Language may be illuminating. It was (in the 1960s) an attempt by some linguists to use the notion of teaching kids to read (from experience in the Soviet Union and Mexico) in their first/own languages, rather than switching them to a national language before teaching them to read. The question was the best way to teach children to read. The notion of Black Language has since transformed into issues of Culture, who owns the language or dialect, and so on. I was involved in the earlier movement as a linguist during the Civil Rights days in the 1960s, on the Board of an organization called the Education Study Center in Washington, D.C., which promoted such ideas, wrote texts, etc.

Probably the greatest victory we won was with promoting and justifying the use of American Sign Language for deaf children. William Stokoe at Gallaudet College (also a member of the Board of the Education Study Center) wrote *the* book on ASL, promoted, gathered, published endless articles and not a few books, and finally was successful in getting the idea of sign language into our thinking, and allowing (not until 1972) deaf kids to use sign language as part of their education. Now ASL is very widely accepted, and the idea of *deaf and dumb* is not an equation that most people make. About a decade ago, we had a battle over the legitimacy of ASL at the University of Minnesota, and won it with the argument that the deaf *are a culture, thus possess the right to use their own language, namely sign language.*.

3. Franz Boas, "Changes in Bodily Form of Descendants of Immigrants (1910-1913)" in *Race, Language, and Culture* (New York: Free Press, 1940). p. 60-75.

4. Many current studies in behavioral, linguistic, and neuroscientific evolution seem to this Boasian-Deweyan to be very anti-progressive, very Social Darwinist attempts to recreate the sense that much/most of life is predetermined, at least not very changeable. This smacks of the sorts of eugenics that Boas fought with his concept of

culture as change --as opposed, usually, to a concept of nature which meant fixed, unchangeable, given, or predetermined.

5. Richard Hofstadter, *Social Darwinism in American Thought.* (Boston: Beacon Press, 1944). The history of Social Darwinism continues. Hofstadter's book accounts for how Spencer's (and Some of Darwin's) ideas were developed in America. They contributed strongly to the eugenics movement which was put into public policy by Hitler, and also led to the anti-immigration bill (Reed-Nelson) of 1924. Many of these ideas resonate today within the notions of predeterminism and evolutionary psychology which are carried under the banner of sociobiology.

6. This essay is written from the perspective of the anthropologist doing fieldwork: consider that these are *notes from the field*! The exotic setting for my fieldwork in this instance has been primarily at and within the University of Minnesota, Minneapolis.

7. Adler, a convert from Judaism to Catholic Thomism, has had an enormous impact on the American psyche, trying to get us invested in the Great Books. As a reader of many of Adler's Great Books, my critique is less of reading them, but in *how* we read them, their power in developing and sustaining particular ideas. This is to say that the history and politics of ideas are very powerful in the world and in our thinking, and the Great Books need to be read carefully and critically. Here, I seem to differ with both the neoconservative and *multiculti* views of literature.

8. The question of Science representing a sense of universal truth is very useful for Humanists to counter claims of religion. While most scientists talk these days about modeling the world, and searching for the most powerful or inclusive explanations, most people (including neo-Conservative academics) take science to be an alternative to religious explanations, seemingly substituting science for a deity which has similar but opposing properties of authority, knowledge, and truth. Here we are also arguing over issues such as reality. I take this moment as one which is propitious for the resurgence of a Pragmatism which returns us more to human experience, rather than being hidden behind polemics which background our experience to mostly methodological considerations. According to Hofstadter (*Social Darwinism in American Life*, chap. 7), Pragmatism arose last century in quite similar circumstance as prevail today: intellectual, but also the dynamics of this moment of money-madness which was called the

Gilded Age last century; leading (as now) to the rise and pressures of monopolies upon the world.

9. Gathered in the National Association of Scholars. I attended a national meeting of the NAS in Minneapolis several years ago, and noted both the content and the contexts (who was there, who was not) in a setting where I personally knew many of attendees and their affiliations. (Call it: participatory observation or ethnological field-work!) A great number of NAS attendees were older white—but also European-ethnic—males; having made it in the academy, they resent and resist the idea of women and persons of color, living and writing in the present, displacing their sense of subject matter: the Great Books, Great Ideas, and Great Thinkers.

10. Jean-François Lyotard, *The Postmodern Condition*. (Min-neapolis: University Minnesota Press, 1984). The major move of postmodernism is to attempt to shift the methods and assumptions of science (external reality, objectivity, and all) to the sense that all is ultimately talk-about or *narrativity* in the discussions, writings, and reports even of scientists. Or the idea that the world is our text is be-ing replaced by the idea that everything is a text, and the rules of in-terpretation and narrativity retake the foundations of knowledge. I worry that this move opens up the idea of theistic texts as being as *reasonable*, correct, and authoritative as any others.

11. The (neo)neoMarxist thinking is in a great deal of flux. The European lit-crits seem to have been assimilated to their thinking: about Freud (and Lacan), that what goes on is heavily affected or shaped by processes of the unconscious, thus not directly available for analysis or understanding; from Saussure, that meaning (and much else) is essentially *arbitrary*, directing us on a slippery slope beyond skepticism toward cynicism and much leaning toward nihilism--againstness, and much undoing--but elegantly and with much word-play. My (mostly quite thoughtful) colleagues do not seem very op-posed to some sorts of return to American Pragmatism, both realizing and admitting that much of the lit-crit ideas were probably developed by Peirce, Dewey, perhaps especially by students of George Herbert Mead and the Chicago School, such as E. Goffman.

12. Bruno Latour and Steve Woolgar, *Laboratory Life* (Beverly Hills: Sage Publications, 1979). This book is a report of a tour of par-ticipatory-observation fieldwork in the Salk Institute. Truth is in the

telling, while the issues of sickness and death, biological organisms moving, seem to form background, eventually to the point of disappearance--since, in this context, telling and representation overwhelm all else.

13. At the forementioned NAS national meeting, I was witness to a discussion of the superiority of male rationality, and happened to mention the Polgar sisters who seem to be quite good chess players. The comment was not well received.

14. E. O. Wilson, *Consilience: The Unity of Knowledge* (New York Alfred A. Knopf, 1998). In many ways this is a direct opposite to Lyotard's attempt to create narrativity as the way to truth and knowledge. Wilson's claims about the uniqueness of human language (p. 131) are directly contrary to Darwin's thinking that language is not *qualitatively* different from the speech of other species. Wilson's stories about the human are in the same but oppositional Platonic metaphysical stance of its oppositional postmodernists: but now, in the name of Science.

15. See H.B. Sarles, *Language and Human Nature* (Minneapolis: University Minnesota Press, 1985) for a critique of this mode of making claims about the uniqueness of language.

16. I've written an extensive analysis of the currents of nihilism in *Nietzsche's Prophecy: The Crisis in Meaning*, to be published by Humanity Books. Whatever humanism offers, it seems not much occupied with the issues of spirituality and searches for meaning which seem to be most attractive to the American population: Alternative Medicine and all that. Staying alive longer in an era where we seem to have given the world of knowledge and information top priority--in the contexts of technological hegemony—doesn't leave us with the sense of direction which a pursuit of wisdom might offer.

17. Bill Readings, *The University in Ruins* (Albany: SUNY Press, 1996).

2

THE CANADIAN EXPERIENCE WITH

MULTICULTURALISM

IS IT RELEVANT ELSEWHERE?

Don Page

Canada's cultural mosaic is often referred to by critics of multicultural policies in the United States who cite the Québec crisis to support their position. Such references are simplistic and misleading, however, and it is the intention here to raise critical issues that these references overlook. Of course there are lessons to be learned from the Canadian experience but care must be taken with the facts and with the logic that flows from them.

The original Canadian constitution (1867) protected both French and English cultures and preserved British treaty obligations protecting the cultural rights of aboriginal groups, now called First Nations. Thus, while the United States opted constitutionally for a unilingual, homogeneous national culture, multilingual multiculturalism has been an imperative in Canada from its beginning. In the first century after confederation, however, Canadian public

English- and French-speaking groups, while the First Nations cultures were virtually disregarded—in fact, often abused. Only within the last three decades have Canada's aboriginal peoples been heard with respect, and at long last public opinion and public policy are reflecting a truly multicultural (as opposed to bicultural) vision of the Canadian state. For reasons that are related, this same period has seen the rise of French ethnic nationalism with its call for independence for the province of Québec. The new multicultural vision can be viewed as the response to this by the liberal majority.

Charles Taylor, the McGill University philosopher and a Québecker, has thought more than most about the politics of multiculturalism. In a widely cited paper,[1] Taylor traces the rise of nationalism and its relationship to the development of Western concepts of freedom and the autonomous individual. He observes that ethnic nationalism is unavoidable when a territorially-based group faces what it perceives to be domination or oppression by another group. Professor Taylor speaks directly from his understanding of the Québec situation in Canada—a situation to which he refers at length. His analysis outlines the various approaches that a liberal democracy can take to issues of multi-ethnicity, and points out the paradoxes and contradictions inherent in each of these approaches. In the end, he argues for a special kind of politics of recognition—and it is clear that his conclusion reflects the Québeckers' perceived need for more formal recognition of their distinctiveness within the Canadian federation. Taylor represents the view of a majority of Canadians if Québeckers themselves are included. However, the implementation of his solution is a political problem in English-speaking Canada, and is the issue at the heart of the country's crisis. It should also be noted that he was writing in 1994 when political support in Québec for separatism was at an all-time high, and when attitudes in the rest of Canada had hardened sufficiently to make separation seem inevitable. With recent political developments, however, this threat has subsided, at least for the near future.

Advocates of multicultural policies should not conclude that Taylor's preferred approach to multiculturalism is applicable in all countries with diverse populations—especially the United States. They should note, for example, that the historic issue of language is critical to the Canadian situation. They should also note the complex relationships that exist between language and education policies, as well as the economic, territorial, and socio-political arrangements that must be in place to reflect these policies. In these arrangements, Canada is very different from the United States.

The Various Multiculturalisms

A new autonomous territory came into being on April 1, 1999, the result of a land claims agreement negotiated by the federal government with its Inuit inhabitants (formerly called Eskimos) who are 80 percent of its population of twenty-five thousand. Comprising most of Canada's high Arctic, it is named Nunavut and its official language is Inuktitut. It is the third largest of Canada's provinces and territories, and it is the least populated. Its elected territorial government is responsible for developing its own natural and economic resources, and for administering health, education and social services, with the right to raise its own taxes; however, using the transfer formula that applies between Ottawa and the provinces and territories—a formula that equalizes social, health and educational standards across the country—it will receive most of its C$620 million budget from Ottawa. It will also administer the Canadian criminal law but will do so within Inuit traditions. Its people will continue to elect representatives to the federal parliament and will be subject to federal laws and taxes. A comparable land claims agreement has more recently been agreed with the Inuit people of Labrador and similar negotiations are in progress with other aboriginal groups.

Considering the special cultural and linguistic characteristics of Québec and Nunavut, it is evident that the multiculturalism discussed so far is territorial and multilingual. Every federal country, including the United States, was originally multicultural in the territorial sense—each state or province comprised a territorially-based population that deemed itself to have characteristics that set it apart from the others at the time it entered federation. With or without official encouragement, however, a national culture develops over time from the values and traditions that are common to all members of the union, and it is with the integrity of this that multiculturalism critics are concerned.

Unlike Canada, the United States has pursued policies to deliberately develop a patriotic and unified national culture.[2] Thus, with a single official language, and notwithstanding the territorially-based minority populations of Hawaii and Alaska, the United States is much less overtly multicultural than Canada. To the outsider, the resulting American nationalistic monoculture suggests a sense of purpose not found in other liberal democracies—and to some, even of cultural arrogance. (Thus Canadians understand the recent vote by the people of Puerto Rico not to apply for U.S. statehood, for fear of losing their culture and language). In the official American[*] unilingual and unicultural arrangement, it would appear the cultures of aboriginal people can only be second-class at best; in contrast, the pluralistic Canadian approach might seem to offer the possibility of accommodating the First Nations cultures

---

[*] "American" is used by author to refer to the United States, and this usage is preserved, along with Canadian spellings. [Ed.]

on a more equal basis. The decision, sensible under the circumstances, by the people of California to insist on English as the language of teaching in their schools suggests that the ideal of homogeneity continues to be widely held by the American public.

Territorial multiculturalism must be differentiated from other kinds. It is immigration, with its resulting intermingling of diverse ethnic groups throughout the population, that is usually discussed in the American context. This "non-territorial" form of cultural diversity is totally different in kind from that discussed above. In 1971, Prime Minister Pierre Trudeau introduced a multicultural policy that was intended to formally acknowledge and celebrate the contributions of the many newer immigrant groups to Canada's cultural diversity. Predictably, the legislation was controversial, and more conservative administrations have since scaled down its original initiatives to encourage immigrant cultural activities. Nevertheless, the policy continues to reinforce the "cultural mosaic" view of Canada, of which its citizens are proud.

Much of the Canadian literature trumpeting Canada's multiculturalism refers to this non-territorial kind, and to the verve it gives to community life. However, it is unlikely that the Canadian experience as a direct result of immigration is very different from that of other immigrant societies—an experience that is usually considered to be positive on balance. Careful studies have shown that immigrants to both English and French Canada participate in the affairs of their host communities, regardless of their origins and whether or not they maintain their original cultural traditions in private; their voting record is similar to the national average. It is also striking that, regardless of ethnic origin, the offspring of immigrants integrate seamlessly into Canadian society, absorbing the history, social values and traditions of the host community. Aside from occasional complaints of racial discrimination,[3] the most noticeable effects at the community level as a result of significant rates of immigration are those that relate to religion—e.g., the appearance of mosques and temples, or the wearing of turbans and headscarves. The issues of language and education that contribute to the results of these studies are dealt with below. A later section will deal with ethical and religious issues.

Besides territorial multiculturalism and that arising from immigration, there is a third category for which both countries make special provisions—it includes groups such as women, visible minorities, gays, etc. Although this third category implies a stretching of the definition of culture, it is usually included in the American discussion by conservative critics of multicultural policies. With some minor exceptions, it is unlikely that the Canadian experience with this category is unique, however, and it will not be discussed further here.

Language and Education Issues in Canada

Although most French-speaking Canadians live in Québec, there are francophone individuals and minority communities in all of the other provinces and territories; only in New Brunswick are francophones (the Acadians) comparable in number to anglophones. The minority population of anglophones in Québec (approximately 10%) must live and work in the French language although they have the right to receive provincial government services in English. Most of the francophones outside Québec live in Ontario and New Brunswick, where they can access provincial government services in French, and where provincial government business is conducted bilingually. In Ontario this bilingualism is granted by custom, while in New Brunswick it is a statutory requirement. In all provinces and territories, court legal proceedings are conducted bilingually on request. It is important to note that very few francophones living outside Québec are in favour of Québec separation.

All federal government business is conducted bilingually, and federal services are available across the country in both languages. Under federal law, all products marketed in Canada must be labeled, and instructions provided, in both English and French. In all parts of the country, public education is available in either French or English where local numbers warrant. Immigrants to Canada must make a language decision when deciding where to live. Since a decision to live in Québec implies a necessity to speak French, the children of immigrants to Québec are required to attend schools where instruction is in French.[4] In the rest of the country, immigrants may choose their working language, although for practical reasons the choice is almost always English. Whether the language of instruction is English or French, teaching of the other language is a requirement in all Canadian schools, and some proficiency in the second language is a normal entry requirement at post-secondary educational institutions.

With the exception of aboriginal groups, there are no public schools in other languages—and it is not conceivable that a demand, or public support, for such could arise. On formally receiving Canadian citizenship, all immigrants swear or affirm allegiance to the Crown,[5] and must have become sufficiently proficient in either English or French to do so. There is a clear undertaking by immigrants to conduct their future public affairs in either English or French, and to educate their children to do likewise. In this respect, therefore, there is no difference between Canada and the United States in their expectations of immigrants with regard to language—except only that in Canada the language can be French.

The Québec Red Herring

Arthur M. Schlesinger, Jr.,[6] John J. Miller,[7] and other conservative critics of multiculturalism in the United States, express concern that multicultural policies lead to a weakening of the "Americanization" process among immigrants, and to a tendency towards social fragmentation. Such claims beg questions about Canada where, unlike the United States, multiculturalism is accepted and celebrated. Those who attribute disharmony in the United States to multiculturalism point to Canada's problems vis-à-vis Québec and conclude or imply, as does Schlesinger, that a parallel exists between these developments in the two countries. On this point they are simplistic—and wrong. They are also wrong when they allege that Canadians generally lack a strong sense of nationalism.

There is no language situation in the United States to parallel that of Québec in Canada, nor can such a situation be envisaged in the future, given the American commitment to unilingualism in its institutions. Those who suggest such a parallel also overlook the territorial factor in the Québec case, again for which there is no American parallel; Hawaii and Alaska are, perhaps, potential territorial parallels, but these are not among the concerns cited by anti-multiculturalists. If a valid comparison with Canada is to be made, it should be done with the English-speaking part of Canada, excluding Québec. When this is done it will be found that "English Canada" does not suffer the kind of social fragmentation that is represented, for example, by black rejectionist groups in the United States; nor, incidentally, is there such fragmentation within Québec society.[8]

Nothing in anglophone Canada or the United States can parallel the very strong pride and commitment that Québeckers feel to their province and culture. Most anglophone Canadians are glad to have this cultural jewel in their federation, and do not want it to separate; but if this should happen, opinion polls consistently show that the commitment of anglophones to Canada will remain strong. Opinion polls also consistently show that up to three-quarters of Québeckers themselves strongly want to retain their Canadian nationality, although about one-third of these would feel forced to support separation if their demand is not met for more formal recognition of the distinct character of their society within the federation.

There is, clearly, a Canadian nationalism that is not detected by Schlesinger and the other American critics who use Canada as an example to support their opposition to multiculturalism. When the "red herring" of the Québec issue is removed, one finds that communal solidarity in Canada remains strong in spite of official multiculturalism.

The Role of Community

Why do American critics of multiculturalism fail to detect the solidarity that is Canadian nationalism? It is obvious that the discussion of multiculturalism in the United States is based on concepts of nationalism and the role of the state that are different from those that prevail in Canada. As has been noted, American national culture has a strong patriotic element that was fostered over generations as a matter of public policy. Perhaps these critics simply assume that communal solidarity is not possible in a diverse and multilingual society without benefit of patriotic pledges of allegiance and the like.

The answer is in cultural differences between Canadians and Americans that are rooted in history.[9] For most of its history English-speaking Canada has been populated mostly by people of British origin, and until the 1950s its majority culture could be considered as an extension of that of the "mother country." Patriotism in Canada was simply a quiet loyalty to the monarch that was taken for granted along with belief in God. Meanwhile, the separate and very conservative Catholic culture of Québec was hardly noticed by its neighbours.

Developments after WWII transformed this picture. The psychological connection with Britain weakened rapidly as trade and immigration patterns changed. By the 1960's, the United States had replaced Britain as Canada's dominant trade and defence partner, and southern Europe had supplanted Britain as a major source of immigrants. Today, immigrants from the Caribbean, south and east Asia, and recently Africa, far outnumber those from Europe.

Three political developments in the 1960s are fundamental to the way Canadians now see themselves. The first was the rise of French ethnic nationalism as Québeckers emancipated themselves from the dominance in their lives of an anglophone business community and the Roman Catholic church. The second was the liberal response to this Québec development, with enactment of radical policies for promoting a truly bilingual and bicultural relationship between Québec and the rest of Canada. The third, and most important, were far-reaching liberal social policy initiatives—the enactment of legislation to remove health care from the marketplace and to make it a universal right of citizenship, and to provide reasonable levels of income security for all Canadians. These developments have led to what has become known officially as the "social union" between the various levels of government—giving a new legitimacy to the cause of federalism across the country. It ensures a common and decent standard of health care and social services by means of transfers of the national wealth from the rich to the poorer regions, and is a major weapon with which to argue the case for Québec to remain a part of Canada.

Today, the British connection is virtually gone, to the extent that pundits predict Canada's withdrawal from the monarchy at the end of the present Queen's reign. The parliamentary form of government is likely to remain, however; Canadians value its relative responsiveness to the citizens' needs, as compared with the American "separation of powers" form of government.

The new "Canadianism" has its roots in the social policy initiatives of the 1960s. They have produced a strong sense of a national community—of social solidarity—that has replaced the old British patriotism. Ironically, the threat from Québec's ethnic nationalism has created an increased awareness by the rest of Canadians of their new patriotism—a patriotism that has little to do with history or military exploits, and everything to do with a sense of community. It is a sense of community that overrides ethnic and linguistic differences, with little to fear from multicultural policies. This new "Canadianism" is obviously different in kind from traditional American patriotism, which may be why Schlesinger and other American authors have not recognized it.

Additional Historical Factors

It should be noted that certain facts of history make the Canadian situation less complex than the American. Foremost is the fact that slavery, with its catastrophic consequences throughout United States history up to and including the present day, was never a socially divisive issue, although it existed in some communities until 1834. Proportionally, there is a much smaller black population in

Canada, and there is no equivalent to the black rejectionist groups which have arisen in the United States. Canada's original blacks were refugees from slavery, but their descendents are now outnumbered by black immigrants from the Caribbean who buoyantly exhibit their culture in annual celebrations in the big cities, to which all are invited.

Another factor that has allowed this new kind of nationalism to take root in Canada is the absence of a history of grand military exploits. There was no Revolution or Civil War to solidify a historic national image. Since the repulse of the American invasions in the War of 1812, all major Canadian military action has taken place abroad in support of allies or in peacekeeping operations. There have been commendable exploits, such as victory at the battle of Vimy Ridge in 1917, or in the Juno Beach sector on D-Day. However, Canadian military history is not glorified and plays little or no part in the country's modern view of itself. Canadians see their armed forces solely in terms of the peacekeeping needs of the United Nations and of their obligations within the North Atlantic Treaty Organization.

Ethical and Religious Issues

Humanists and others are concerned with the relentless pressures of certain religious groups to impose their cultural values on the whole of society—on issues such as abortion and school prayer.[10] Experience in Canada suggests that these pressures are diluted as religious diversity increases with immigration. For example, although the traditional Christian calendar is still followed for major holidays in public schools, the religious carols and nativity stories of Christmas have given way to secular replacements, out of respect for the greater religious diversity that now exists in the community. There is a sense of loss among Christians, but most parents appear to accept the end of these traditions in the schools in the spirit of tolerance that is needed for social harmony.

The limits on how far Canadian society is prepared to bend to accommodate the conflicting values and traditions of immigrant groups are being tested constantly, however. An early test came in Alberta with a Sikh recruit for the Royal Canadian Mounted Police who insisted on being permitted to wear a turban instead of the traditional "mountie" hat. It took a court decision to confirm his right to do so; as a result, Sikhs who choose to do so now may wear turbans in all police forces and in the armed forces—and after more than a decade, it is no longer an issue. A more difficult recent case involved a Sikh schoolboy in British Columbia who was sent home for wearing the traditional Sikh dagger, a religious symbol worn on the leg. He was ordered back to school by a judge with the condition that he wrap and secure the weapon in such a way that it is always hidden and not readily accessed. The school board decided not to appeal what was felt to be a reasonable compromise.

Another turban issue arose with the case of an east Indian immigrant who had fought with the British army, and who wished to assert his right to join the Royal Canadian Legion. He was denied entry to his local branch in Vancouver while wearing a turban (the headgear with which he fought) and the case required pressure from national Legion headquarters before his right of entry was acknowledged. Headgear has also been an issue in several cases involving Muslim schoolgirls wearing headscarves which were deemed by school boards not to accord with their dress codes. Today, it is commonplace to see headscarves in high schools across the country.

Humanists should have no problem with the above cases where serious ethical issues are not involved. More difficult is the situation with some immigrant women who choose to have abortions on the basis of fetal sex determination tests; among certain Eastern cultures, it appears that boy babies are more desirable than girl babies. This is a community concern because abortions are paid for by the taxpayer through the universal medicare system. It is expected that this and other situations of its type will be addressed by the medical profession.

Another class of problem is raised by the predicament of young persons who, wishing to choose their own marriage partners, come into conflict with the traditions of their parents. Of course, in such situations the solution must clearly lie with the young people themselves, and it is interesting to note that most are choosing to break with their parents' tradition.

Experience in Canada shows that the great majority of immigrants fit in well with the host community. They enter the workforce at all levels or they go into business. They are law-abiding. Their children attend the local schools and soon learn to speak and act like other Canadian children. There is no evidence of the basic values of the host community having to change or bend to accommodate those of immigrant groups. Those infrequent clashes that occur are usually associated with an immigrant's religion, as in the above examples. The majority of these problems are resolved successfully at the community level; certainly, the more intractable problems can be, and are being, handled by the courts guided by Canadian law and the Charter of Rights.

Postscript: A Disagreement about Culture

A recent book by American economist Tyler Cowan provides an interesting counterpoint to this discussion. Entitled *In Praise of Commercial Culture,*[11] it argues against the Canadian positions on issues of culture that are currently in dispute between Canada and the United States under terms of the North American Free Trade Agreement. Both Canada and Mexico have taken strong positions to exempt culture from the terms of NAFTA but, predictably, problems have arisen with definitions. The dispute involves rules for American magazines entering Canada. The details of the issue are complex; it is sufficient here to note that there are threats of retaliatory embargoes against Canadian products entering the United States if Ottawa enacts a new law that Parliament has passed with wide multi-party support.[12]

Cowan voices the position taken by U.S. negotiators—that the marketplace should determine the development of culture. This position misses the Canadian point—that Canadian writers must have the opportunity to express Canadian perspectives, and that government has an overall regulatory role to play to ensure that such opportunities exist. The dispute highlights a crucial difference between Canadian and American perspectives on culture. Unlike Americans, Canadians insist on shielding their culture from the whims of the marketplace, as they have done with health care. In common with Europeans and others, Canadians appear to be less inclined than Americans to accept the consequences of social and economic Darwinism.

Notes

1. Charles Taylor, *Multiculturalism: Examining the Politics of Recognition* (Princeton: Princeton University Press, 1994).

2. An example, among many, of the differences is the absence in Canada of anything like the pledge of allegiance that takes place in the United States. Canadians do not think of their flag or country in this way, and many would find it unseemly to make such a public display.

3. The serious racial events that occur in Canada usually involve First Nations people.

4. Critics of this Québec language policy regarding its immigrants should consider its direct parallel with the decision of the people of California to use only English as the language of instruction in their schools.

5. This is the only oath or pledge of allegiance they are ever likely to encounter. Indeed, the great majority of citizens who have their citizenship from birth never encounter such an oath unless they contract to work for the Crown (the government).

6. Arthur M. Schlesinger, Jr., *The Disuniting of America: Reflections on a Multicultural Society*, 2nd ed. (New York: W. W. Norton, 1998).

7. John J. Miller, *The Unmaking of Americans: How Multiculturalism has Undermined America's Assimilation Ethic* (New York: Free Press, 1970).

8. The anglophone community in Québec might be considered an exception since it opposes separation from Canada. It is still unclear how this community will react if separation occurs.

9. These differences were discussed by the author in an earlier article, "Why Are We So Different? A Canadian view," *Humanism Today* 11 (1997), pp. 133-154.

10. For humanists, this and other such areas of concern are addressed by their social objective to achieve the Open Society—a concept which is fundamental to the humanist perspective.

11. Tyler Cowan, *In Praise of Commercial Culture* (Cambridge: Harvard University Press, 1998).

12. Since this was written (1999), a compromise has been agreed in this dispute that recognizes the essential Canadian position. Experience suggests, however, that similar cultural differences will continue to feature in relations between Canada and the United States.

3

HUMANISM AND MULTICULTURALISM

A CRITIQUE

Sarah W. Oelberg

A few weeks ago, just as I was preparing to tackle this topic by demonstrating how humanism was poised to take on a leadership role in working for true multiculturalism in the next millennium, I received an e-mail from an esteemed colleague who said he wanted to learn more about humanism. He confessed that his general impression of humanism was positive, but that he also saw it as "anthropocentric, sexist, classist, and racist to its core." He wondered if I could steer him to any readings that would dispel these notions. He also wondered how, if his perceptions were true, I could remain a humanist.

I took up his challenge with aplomb, determined to show him the error of his thinking. I looked at Manifestos, at writings of humanists both early and late, at critiques of humanism, at humanist magazines and journals, and I found—almost nothing. Yes, there are some wonderful words about humanists "concern for the welfare of...all who are neglected or ignored by society," and that we "deplore racial, religious, ethnic or class antagonisms," and we are "critical of sexism or sexual chauvinism." Humanists hold that

> the principle of moral equality must be furthered through elimination of all discrimination based upon race, religion, sex, age, or national origin. This means equality of opportunity and recognition of talent and merit.

And, generously, we declare that

> if individuals are unable to contribute to their own betterment, then society should provide means to satisfy their basic economic, health, and cultural needs.[1]

Generally, this is what I found in my research—a lot of high, moral-sounding language about human rights, equal opportunities, justice, and a little mercy. Precious little about how such worthy goals could be accomplished, and even less about the role of humanism in reaching these ideals. A lot about what ought to be; very little about how to make it so. There is a tremendous difference between "deploring" something, or being "critical" or "concerned" about something, and actually being actively engaged in improving things. I found myself agreeing, to some degree, with another friend who claims that humanists love the idea of humanity more than humanity itself; that humanism is shallow, ineffective in accomplishing its aims, and self-congratulatory.

How could I answer my colleague's claim that humanism is anthropocentric, sexist, classist and racist? Interestingly, (to me) the easiest of these to dispel was the charge of being anthropocentric. Humanism has, of course, come across that way, and for good reason. But it is not too difficult to make the case that our anthropocentrism makes us the friends of other living creatures and the world itself, for we recognize that humans are the ones who do harm, and must also work to make things better. Humans may be the center of the universe, or the top of the ladder, or whatever, but that puts us in precisely the right position to begin to understand

and address the interdependence of all being. This might make a good future topic.

As to his other charges, which are more related to the topic of multiculturalism, I had more difficulty countering his claims. In my attempt to do so, I found the focus of my ideas for this paper changing, until now I see it as a critique of humanism with regard to its readiness to take a leadership role in fostering multiculturalism. And, I see multiculturalism as much more than a mingling of many cultures, languages, races, and ethnic groups. For true multiculturalism to prevail, such mingling must be on equal terms; one group cannot be more powerful or acceptable than any other group. In America, this means that we have a lot of preliminary work to do in fighting racism and oppression, especially of African Americans, but to some extent, all minority groups. The question, then, becomes: "How well are humanists poised to tackle the difficult issues of race and inequality?"

I cannot argue with my colleague's observation about humanism and sexism. For many years I tried to convince myself that all of the humanist literature which used the word "man" exclusively was only a matter of the grammar of the time, and it really meant all humans. As I have become more involved in humanist circles, and less willing to accept things at face value, I have come to realize that often, although not always, the word "man" was meant to mean just that, and no more. Every woman in the humanist movement, even today, can tell stories of male-centeredness and feeling left out, ignored, and dismissed. We still have a long, long, way to go on this issue even among ourselves. But again, I don't think that is what I want to address in this paper. Maybe another time.

Classism, for sure. We are guilty as charged. Our emphasis on the use of reason; our love of intellectual pursuits and arguments; our way of being together (expensive meetings at fancy hotels); our organizational structures (pay your dues, or you can't belong); and many other things contribute to our being classist, and elitist.

We do not like to think that of ourselves, but it is true. Still again, class is not really a cultural issue, although it is certainly related, so I am not going to focus on it. However, as many claim, there is a high correlation between class and race, so much of what I will say about race will also pertain to class.

That brings us to the harshest charge of all—that we are racist. This is what I would like to concentrate on in this paper. I will pretty much limit my remarks to racism, else I get mired in the morass of many different cultures and issues, and lose focus. And, by racism, I will be talking mostly about the issues related to black-white relations and realities, while acknowledging that the problem is much broader than that, and much of what will be said would also apply to other groups.

There are, of course, many different kinds and levels of racism. Some is quite obvious and overt, such as name calling; most is more subtle, like a teacher notifying white students' parents when the student is not doing well, but not black parents, or a good liberal telling an African American, "You are very articulate and knowledgeable." Individual racism refers to prejudice and feelings of superiority over another race; institutional racism relates to institutional practices and policies that perpetuate racial inequities. Interpersonal racism has to do with the amount of cross-racial contact people have; societal racism is when the constructs of a society are such that it is very difficult for the races to mix, especially in unplanned, everyday encounters. Occasional racism is when an incident happens which is considered unusual; systemic racism is there all the time, throughout the system, and affects the lives of minorities every day.

As humanists, we purport to care about issues of prejudice, discrimination, inequality, and injustice. A rather extensive and useless discussion has emerged in recent years about how to have humanism itself become more diverse. We have examined ourselves and our policies, declared ourselves "open" and unprejudiced, and decided it must be because African Americans don't want to associate with us, or don't like what we have to offer. But that's okay, we tell ourselves—most white Americans don't either. Whenever someone suggests that we might consider changing how we do things, maybe "loosen up a little" and sing some spirituals, or change where we hold our meetings, that person is usually told that we should not compromise our principles in some vain hope that minorities would join us. Then, we would have to ask ourselves: "Why did they join? For what humanism is, or for the concessions we made?" That usually ends any productive discussion on the issue.

There are two levels at which we need to address racism in the United States. (Actually, there are more, but two are all I am going to discuss). The first is the interpersonal level, which includes how we as individuals seek out opportunities to be with and relate to other groups, how we intentionally interact in ways which are designed to further cross-racial understanding, and how we become a truly open and diverse community of humanism. I would suggest that we have trouble in these interpersonal areas because most of us are middle-upper-middle class, work in professions where minorities are rare, live in areas which are pretty exclusive, socialize with "our own kind", and attend largely segregated churches, clubs, or other organizations. In other words, our lives do not easily and automatically interface with the lives of a significant number of African Americans. And, even when they are in proximity, we do not relate to them in the same ways that we do with whites. This is not necessarily a function of being humanists, although there is certainly a high correlation between humanism and class, education level, profession, etc. The question is: Why does not our humanist stance with regard to the worth and dignity of all people require us to make extraordinary efforts to interface more meaningfully with other groups?

The other level of racism is the societal, and here is where humanists ought to be deeply involved. This requires dismantling the systemic and institutional constructs which foster and perpetuate racism and all that goes along with it, like poverty, injustice, and isolation. Virtually every institution in America which affects the lives of minorities and under which they have to live, is controlled by whites. With that control comes power, and with power comes oppression, and that is what institutional racism is all about. Since these controlling institutions work to our advantage, we tend to assume they work the same for everyone. They don't. What advantages us disadvantages others; what serves the privileged disserves the underprivileged.

Allow me one example. Most of us are probably somewhat concerned with making socially responsible investments. We have excised from our portfolios stocks of companies that produce dangerous products, or sell to the wrong countries, or pollute the environment, and so on. But have we looked at the companies in terms of their contributions to racism? For example, does a bank in which you own stock or place your money discriminate in giving loans—especially real estate and agricultural loans? Does it clandestinely support "red-lining"? Does it charge different interest rates to different kinds of clients? Does it have checking accounts which require "minimum" deposits or balances, and charge hefty fees if the amount goes below that? Are its fees for services so onerous that poor people cannot afford to use them? Ironically, if you have a lot of money, it is easy to get free checking and other services; if you do not, you may have to resort to money exchanges, and give over a portion of your pay check just to cash it, and more to get it into mailable form.

As individual humanists, we can become informed about many institutional racist practices, and choose whether to use them or try to change them. But what about humanism as a movement? In general, I find the prospects of humanism being very effective in addressing institutional oppression and racism rather bleak. In spite of our positions on various social issues, we come up wanting when it comes to implementing plans and putting our efforts into meaningful directions. There are several reasons for this, which fall into two categories—practical and ideological.

Practical Limits to Humanist Effectiveness

First, the practical. One reason why humanists cannot be very effective in forcing social change is because we are so fragmented. Instead of one big humanist organization, or movement, we are divided up into several tiny ones. Worse, we spend a lot of time and energy fighting amongst ourselves over relatively unimportant questions like: Is humanism secular or religious? We continue to split ourselves along meaningless fault lines, practically assuring that we will never become united enough to make a difference in the world. Without the equivalent of a denomination, our little humanist societies must act alone, and they are too small to be effective.

Second, humanism is too much embedded in and dependent upon the very institutions and structures which perpetuate racism. By and large, we are the elite, the oppressors, the silent majority. Our comfortable lives would be very upset were things to really change. We attend schools, work at jobs, depend upon businesses and institutions which, in turn, depend upon the perpetuation of racism. We are so much a part of the system that we cannot separate ourselves from it, observe it objectively and dispassionately, and then choose to change it.

Third, we do not play with others very well. Having invested so much into articulating our differences with other religions and even social action organizations, we have difficulty parking our high humanist ideals at the door and getting into the down and dirty work with others. Let's face it—the kind of social justice work we espouse is largely being done by other religious organizations. If we cannot forget how much more "theologically advanced" we are than they, and meet on neutral ground for a larger purpose, we will continue, deservedly, to be left out of the action. This is no longer a question of what we believe should be done to and for oppressed peoples; it is about what we can do with them and with other groups that are working for the same goals.

If these words seem harsh, I mean them to be. The good news, however, is that these practical obstacles to humanism being effective in combating racism and social injustice can be overcome. We can decide that we love humanity enough to put our differences aside and coalesce around this important work. But we will have to change some of our attitudes and language before it can happen.

Ideological Limits to Humanist Effectiveness

What will be much more difficult to deal with are what I call the ideological obstacles to effective anti-racism efforts by humanists. These are things that are so much a part of how we define ourselves that to "give them up" might compromise our humanism. Yet, as I see it, if we are really to make any progress in fighting racism at all levels, we might need to "give up" some of our sacred tenets, or at least "give in" a little. For it is these very ideals which render us suspect to many minorities, who see them as barriers to full cooperation and our ability to "walk in their shoes" and do what is necessary to effect meaningful change.

What are these inherent humanist obstacles? Our devotion to reason, our love of individualism, our strong support of free speech, our commitment to tolerance, our belief that all people are equal and have inherent worth and dignity, and our preference for integration, rather than separation. For different reasons, each of these humanist stances raises suspicion among the African American community. We need to understand why this is so before we can even begin to work with them in a united effort to abolish racism.

Reason

First, our devotion to reason. It is not the use of reason as a tool that is the problem; it is using it exclusively, and setting it above any and all other modes of determining truth that causes discomfort among many, especially minorities. Humanism has taken the concept of reason and placed it above all other hermeneutical tools, until there is little acknowledgment that there are other ways to know the world. For example, Ken Phifer claims "reason, thought and the human mind are the best ways of discovering truth and promoting justice."[2] The AHA says, "Humanism sees science and reason as the best tools for the discovery of knowledge and the achievement of goals."[3] And the San Jose chapter of AHA claims that "We gather insights from all cultures—testing them by the standards of reason and science."[4] *Manifesto I* does insist that "the way to determine the existence and value of all realities is by means of intelligent inquiry."[5] *Manifesto II* says, "Reason and intelligence are the most effective instruments humankind possesses:"[6] Paul LaClair observes that "Humanists believe our discussions and our behavior toward each other must be founded in reason...in our dealings with others...we are obligated to employ reason."[7] And the new "Humanist Manifesto 2000" continues this devotion to reason:

> Humanists recommend that we use reason in framing our ethical judgments....Human values and principles can best be justified in the light of reflective inquiry. Where differences exist we need to negotiate them...by rational dialogue.[8]

Reason is a concept which came from the Enlightenment. The Enlightenment paradigm was that what agreed with reason was deemed worthy; what contrasted with reason was discarded as irrational. While reason was an amazingly effective corrective to the excesses of its time, it is less effective in dealing with a postmodern, multicultural, pluralist world view. It has become, in the eyes of many, its own excess. Like the use of the word "man," Reason is no longer a value-neutral concept. Instead, it can be used to invalidate other ways of knowing in the world, and thereby to effectively oppress any who use other tools, like experience, understanding, wisdom, and even intuition. What race, class, and gender privileges are maintained or enforced by our claim that reason is the most trustworthy method for discovering truths? How does our virtual worship of reason set us apart from those who find their meaning through other modes?

The problem is that humanists are so absolutist about the use of reason. If we claimed that it was one way among many, the one which we prefer, but that we are open to other modes and methods, that would be all right. It would not denigrate those who choose and use other methods, and it would not negate our using them ourselves. Reason is only one function of the mind among many. Emotion, creativity, intuition, and other less linear aspects are what make us fully human. As Richard Erhardt says:

> To hold up one aspect of our being as more fully human than the others is to create an unnecessary hierarchy within the human soul. Are persons, peoples and cultures that give equal weight to the emotional or the intuitional aspects of our nature less fully human than those who rely on rationality alone? If rationality is the "better" way to be human then it stands to good reason that those who are more rational are "better" humans than those who are not. This is implied in the pseudo-intellectualism that pushes reason above all other forms of knowing and reflecting.

> This is the rationale behind racist thinking. It is the rationale behind sexist thinking. It is the rationale behind classist thinking. According to these lines of reasoning, there is a hierarchy of human worth and those who are higher up in the perceived hierarchy are more valuable than those who are lower down....The overvalue placed on reason, its high location in the hierarchy, does have the effect of lessening the humanity of peoples and cultures that place less reliance on the rational. [9]

The humanist devotion to reason also has the effect of lessening the opportunities for and effectiveness of dialogue with oppressed groups. First, because the primary institution which works for social and civil rights is the Christian church. The civil rights movement came from and was dependent upon churches. Much of what happened was not "rational," but it worked because it was heartfelt—emotional, if you will. So in order for humanists to become fully engaged in the work of anti-racism and anti-oppression, we might have to enter into venues we find uncomfortable.

Second, our devotion to reason works against us because what we find to be reasonable, from our exalted position, is often seen as unreasonable by oppressed people, whose experiences have been very different. Some things cannot be approached solely through reason in a society which is inherently unreasonable. Minorities know that, and they resent our pretending that reason is the best way to approach problems. Their experiences in the world have led them to some instant knowledge, not based on reason, but often on survival.

Third, the postmodern attack on the Enlightenment and its critique of humanism raises some valid points. If we are to be completely honest, we have to admit that an exclusive belief in the centrality of reason can lead to its potential misuse as mere rationalization; leading to "excuses," or reasons to accept, or at least not to resist, what could be called "structures of evil." There are some who would claim that reason can, and has, become an instrument of control and oppression. This has been most prevalent in suggestions that reason has been misapplied to have the result of making humanists complicit in supporting the prevailing economic system in this country, which in itself is oppressive and unjust. In an effort to sum up the postmodernist case against Enlightenment/humanist reason, Patricia Waugh writes:

Enlightenment reason...is seen to clarify a world which it has set up in its own terms, in a disguised manifestation of a will to power which secures itself through an insidious exclusion of all that it identifies as non-rational: desire, feeling, sexuality, femininity, art, madness, criminality, non-Caucasian races, particular ethnicities. Reason, even in its Enlightenment mode, is thus seen as part of the grand impulse to control and subjugate which is the logic of capitalism and which has led to the violent forms of oppression in the modern world: imperialism, colonialism, racism, sexism, destruction of the environment, automatization of human beings for the purposes of efficiency. Economic affluence in the West is seen to be dependent upon exploitation elsewhere.[10]

If these seem like harsh words, and they are, let me point out that Waugh is not alone in expressing such a viewpoint. It is not the purpose of this paper to argue with such sentiments, but rather to point out that they are widely enough held to make it increasingly difficult for humanists who continue to bind themselves unwaveringly to the rationalist stance to be taken seriously when they also try to make the claim that they are working for justice, equality, anti-racism and anti-oppression. We need to engage in some self-examination, and determine why this view is so widely held, and if there might be some truth in it which would suggest a modification in our stance and approach.

Fourth, and finally, oppressed people are beyond wanting "reasons" why they are oppressed, and admonitions to "be reasonable." This often feels to them like "blaming the victim," which is often the case. Oppressed people are looking for "friends" who they can trust to understand and empathize with their position, and work along with them to rectify injustices. They need people on their side who are there because of their shared humanness, who are willing to be fully human with them and make a concerted effort to empathasize with their situation—not analyze it, but enter into it.

Perhaps humanists need to strike a balance between an approach which relies solely on a reason which can be seen as critical and rationalizing, and adopt a more "humane" reason that is less strident and more compassionate; a reason which accepts the many different ways of being human. We need to recognize that placing too much value on reason can be perceived as having the effect of lessening the humanity of other peoples and cultures that place less reliance on reason. The human approach requires first engaging people in their space, then using whatever approaches are available to solve the serious problems of racism and oppression in our society.

Individualism

Another central humanist value which is perceived negatively in modern society and in regard to being fully engaged in anti-racism work is our belief in "the preciousness and dignity of the individual person." At first, this seems strange. After all, is it not our affirmation of the worth and dignity of all peoples that positions us to be engaged in anti-racism work? Yes—and no. It is the emphasis on individual person that raises red flags to minorities, who are used to being told, "I am not prejudiced; I like you," only to then experience considerable discrimination directed at them because they are members of a particular race. There is a need to differentiate between individual feelings and societal responses; between selecting out individuals as acceptable and mistreating an entire group.

Another humanist holdover from the Enlightenment, our emphasis on individual autonomy has served us well in our struggle to differentiate our peculiar humanist views from other, more popular ideas. Our individualist attitude supported our absolute freedom to think as we would, and it undergirded our belief in the "self-sufficiency" of humans, which was important to the pursuit of our independent and unpopular path. It supported our belief in the ability of persons to accomplish great things, and it fed our optimism about the ultimate triumph of humankind. In these respects, it has informed much of what we as humanists have accomplished, and it is a valuable precept.

It serves less well, however, in the domain of serious anti-racism and anti-oppression work, for several reasons. First, from the very beginning of the right of freedom of conscience, other

"Rights of Man" were joined to this basic right, including, (and I believe Max Weber claimed especially) the right to pursue one's own economic interests, which included, to John Locke and others, the right to individual property. Freedom and conscience and freedom of enterprise were inextricably connected. The problem, then, lies in the fact that the free pursuit of individual economic gain has served to make for vast inequities in wealth. Those who are living in poverty, who see us dismantling an already inadequate welfare system, and who (often because of race) cannot get decent jobs that will support their families, do not see the "right" to pursue individual economic interests as a right that pertains to them in the same way it does to the more advantaged. Such people are rightfully suspicious of claims of individualism. It is, in a sense, a meaningless right, or one which is used as a "club" to accuse them of making their own difficulties—after all, don't they have the right to be successful? Of course, if other factors, such as race, are intervening in a negative way, economic rights are never equal.

Further, economic individualism, which makes no distinctions between individuals other than monetary ones, destroys the social fabric that would hold people together. It puts people in competition, it establishes "strata" in society based on wealth, and it undermines all other distinctions between people. Those less advantaged, or those "outside" the American economy, quite justifiably accuse us of measuring the "worth" of the individual in monetary terms, not human ones. And, they sneer, "worth and dignity go together, so if we have insufficient monetary worth, we must also have insufficient dignity." If humanists really believed in the innate human worth and dignity of all people they would do much more to assure that everyone lives a life with enough "worth" to allow dignity.

Another problem with individualism is that it tends to counter community, solidarity, and the sense of being members of the same body. If we start from an ontological individualism—the idea that individuals are foremost—then society becomes secondary. But oppressed people need to believe that we are in this thing together, that we need each other, that we will unite in confronting the evils of racism, oppression, and inequality. They know that their precious and unique selves are not going to be able to overcome these evils alone. They need the help and cooperation of those in positions of power.

In fact, there is much evidence that the "me" society, which arose from individualism, has contributed significantly to the exacerbation of problems of race, class, poverty, and oppression. Humans, along with other animals, are fundamentally relational creatures; they need social interaction and a social fabric to instruct their young, provide role models, care for one another, etc. The breakup of extended families into smaller nuclear families began the breakdown of society; the further breakup into one-parent families increased it. Even the youth who are left without the support of a society and extended family which provided the rules, care, example and support they need are aware of the value of not being alone—that is why they join gangs. This is only one of the enormous cultural consequences of ontological individualism, religious or secular, that our society is now having to deal with.

Humanists are going to have to confront the results of our focus on individualism. I believe the increasing diversity in America, and the growing gap between the "haves" and the "have-nots" is going to require that we shift our paradigm from individualism to interdependence; from the autonomy of the individual person to the community of all persons. It is the relational aspects of our common lives that may have the potential to transform society. But we cannot devote ourselves to community only when, and if, it meets our needs, or sustains our interests.

Here I admit to being influenced by Robert Bellah. In his speech to the Unitarian Universalist General Assembly in 1998, Bellah said "I am convinced that only a social understanding of human nature is ontologically true, and that only a social ontology could divert American culture from the destructive course upon which it seems to be set."

He claims that the devotion to individualism easily leads to the idea that we are nothing more than self-interest maximizers. What we have to realize, he said, is that "the sacredness of the individual depends ultimately on our solidarity with all being, not on the vicissitudes of our private selves."

Much of what I am claiming to be detriments to humanism playing a major role in dismantling racism and fighting oppression is due to the way oppressed people interpret our principled stance, and see it as either irrelevant or contrary to what they feel is needed. I am not suggesting that we abandon reason, or forget about individualism. These are valuable precepts in their own right—and in the right place and time. But I have found it very interesting and enlightening to be around my African American daughter's circle of friends, and to see things through their eyes, and to read what black authors have said on similar subjects.

Before I leave the area of individualism and individual worth and dignity, I would like to add one more voice—that of Cornel West. In his book *Race Matters*, he chastises both liberals and conservatives, for different reasons. But of liberals, he says that they are unable, partly because of their focus on individual worth and dignity and their optimism about humanity's future, to recognize what West claims is the most basic issue now facing black America: the nihilistic threat to its very existence. This threat goes beyond economic deprivation and political powerlessness; it is the "profound sense of psychological depression, personal worthlessness, and social despair so widespread in black America."[11] He accuses liberals of showing no understanding of the structural character of culture, and being afraid to talk honestly about culture and the realm of meanings and values.

Like Bellah, West believes that a cause of black nihilism, which results in a numbing detachment from others and a self-destructive disposition toward the world, is the breakdown of social structures and supportive community. The genius of black foremothers and fathers, West claims, was their ability to

> create powerful buffers to ward off the nihilistic threat, to equip black folk with cultural armor to beat back the demons of hopelessness, meaninglessness, and lovelessness. These buffers consisted of cultural structures of meaning and feeling that created and sustained communities...that embodied values of service and sacrifice, love and care, discipline and excellence.[12]

These sustaining communities were largely found in the black churches.

But humanists have difficulty with the theology, emotionality, and emphasis on a better life in the "next" world that are so basic to black churches. We are, all too often, unable to see beyond these characteristics which seem so anti-rational and even alien to us. Thus we cannot appreciate the value of this particular cultural community in sustaining familial and communal networks of support for oppressed black Americans. Further, our preference for "integration" has contributed to a fracturing of even this stalwart black institution, leaving people even more alone and abandoned. Add to this the market-driven shattering of black civil society—and more and more black people are left with little sense of self and fragile existential moorings.

We humanists need to examine the extent to which our philosophy and attitudes toward black churches is complicit in this. As West says

> nihilism is not overcome by arguments or analysis; it is tamed by love and care. Any disease of the soul must be conquered by a turning of one's soul...through one's own affirmation of one's worth—an affirmation fueled by the concern of others.[13]

We cannot both affirm the worth of black Americans and at the same time dismiss and denigrate the very social structure which is the most effective antidote to black nihilism. And perhaps we should further recognize that it is necessary, desirable, and understandable for blacks to want to remain in their own churches, even if, philosophically, they might be humanists, since the black church is the only lasting institution under which African Americans live that they control. Actually, it makes more sense for whites to join black churches to foster integration; then the leadership remains in the hands of blacks.

Freedom of Speech

Now I would like to turn to another of the basic tenets of humanism which is viewed differently by many African Americans. That is our strong support of civil rights, especially the right to free speech. Now African Americans, probably more than any other group, believe in civil rights. They fully realize that any diminishment in anyone's civil rights would also lead to a decrease in their civil rights. They acknowledge the gains they have made by using civil rights as a weapon against their oppressors. They have been, and continue to be, allies in the fight for individual and group rights in America.

However, times have changed, and there is now a serious resurgence of violent hate speech, which has been proven to be a contributing factor in violent hate crimes. There is a growing body of scholars from oppressed groups espousing what they call "critical race theory." Basically, using the idea that every person has worth and dignity, critical race theorists claim that as long as some persons and groups are attacked with hate speech and actions, they are being denied their worth and dignity. They argue that the "experts" are the people being assaulted, and their experience is that racist messages harm real people, and when the legal system offers no redress for that real harm, it perpetuates racism.

In the book, *Words that Wound*, Richard Delgado says:

A racial insult is always a dignitary affront, a direct violation of the victim's right to be treated respectfully. Our moral and legal systems recognize the principle that individuals are entitled to treatment that does not denigrate their humanity through disrespect for their privacy or moral worth.[14]

Charles Lawrence, in the same book, points out that "it is a sad irony that the first instinct of many civil libertarians is to express concern for the possible infringement of the assailant's liberties while barely noticing the constitutional rights of the assailed."[15]

He claims that face-to-face insults, like fighting words, are undeserving of first amendment protection because they have immediate injurious impact, and they violate the intent of the first amendment, which is to promote speech. Because they are felt as attacks, the victims' response is silence, flight or fight, but not dialogue.

In general, the book criticizes ardent civil libertarians for failing to comprehend both the nature and the extent of injury inflicted by racist speech, as well as the long-term consequences in loss of self-worth, fear, and the message given by protecting racist speech that it is all right to be a racist. There is a very fine line between verbal assault and physical assault. The authors call for a reconsideration of the balance that must be struck between our concerns for racial equality and freedom of expression.

Furthermore, whites who fight for free speech need to understand that when they decide that racist speech must be tolerated because of the importance of protecting even unpopular speech, they are asking blacks to bear a terrible burden for the good of society; and, since this burden is imposed on blacks without their consent, it amounts to white domination, pure and simple. When both public and private responses to racist speech are rejected as contrary to the principle of free speech, "it is no wonder that the victims of racism do not consider first amendment absolutists as allies."[16]

Not to belabor the point, I will just say that there are many compelling arguments in this book, and elsewhere, that suggest that there are at least two ways to look at free speech, and blacks view it as contributory to racism. Therefore, they have difficulty with our strong stance protecting all kinds of speech. Again, I am not suggesting that our stance is wrong, or even that it hshould be changed; I am simply pointing out that what we see as high moral positions can be seen very differently by those who are experiencing racism and oppression.

Tolerance

Another word that humanists love to use is "tolerance," and it is also a world that has come to have some negative meanings, especially to those who feel that the people in power merely "tolerate" them. When oppressed people read of our humanist "commitment to tolerance," they perceive it as another kind of hierarchy, for if one group is tolerant of another, there is a kind of presumption that the tolerant group is somehow preferable, even superior, to the group they are tolerant toward. What we are saying, to them, when we claim to be "tolerant," is that we don't really think another group is as good as we are, but, because we are liberal and tolerant, we will forgive them for being who they are, and let them live their lives in peace.

The dictionary offers some very positive meanings for tolerance, like "open-minded" and "broad-minded." But it also suggests "bear with," "endure," "put up with," "accept," and "abide" as synonyms. Unfortunately, these more negative definitions are how many minorities feel we mean the word. Tolerance often implies a distaste for the characteristics or actions of the other. It may also imply a power differential. In order to feel true kinship, we have to go beyond mere tolerance of those who are different than we, to actually connecting with them as equals. Tolerance is somehow short of recognizing that our common humanity means that we have a bond which, while acknowledging our differences, and limitations, also celebrates, respects, embraces and affirms our humanness.

There is another way in which tolerance is not necessarily a sign of good will, and that is when it is used to excuse things like sexual harassment, racist acts, assault, or other oppressive actions. Again, some minorities equate liberalism with this kind of tolerance. There should be limits to our tolerance; violations of another's human rights should not be tolerated. I suggest that we need to review how we intend and act upon the principle of tolerance—both ways. I believe we need to go beyond tolerance and use words such as understanding, valuing, respect, solidarity, affirmation, and empowerment. Ultimately, change will occur if we follow those words with practices which encourage awareness, dialogue, justice, and equality, and actions aimed at developing a caring and critical community. I am not sure how much longer we can get away with tolerating mere tolerance.

Integration

The final word, or ideal, that appears in the Manifestos and in much of humanist thought is "integration." This, too, has outlived its usefulness, and brands us as suspect to many minorities. The new concept, as we recognized when choosing this topic, is "multiculturalism." There is a rather large difference in the meaning of these two words. Integration was a fine concept at the time of segregation; it was a significant improvement and a necessary step in achieving equality in race relations. But in this new age of diversity of many cultures, it has negative overtones.

Integration implies a blending together of different groups to create some kind of unified whole. It has always, however, had an implicit meaning that "outside" groups would be integrated into the existing majority culture, and would have to learn to adjust to it. It also presumed that the minority culture would no longer exist as a separate entity, or even an identifiable culture. It implied homogenization. And it has been shown to have serious limitations. Although integration espoused acceptance and inclusion, it did not necessarily feel welcoming to those who had been excluded and marginalized in the past. There was always a tension that the integrated group felt; that their acceptance was conditional upon their "fitting in" adequately.

Minorities felt like they were always the ones who had to change, adjust, and give up their identity. A survey conducted for the National Conference of Christians and Jews in 1994 discovered that, although different minority groups harbor strong negative feelings and prejudices against each other, they are united in their feelings toward white Americans. The poll showed that decidedly negative views of white Americans were shared by a majority of African Americans, Latino Americans and Asian Americans. They perceive white people as "bigoted, bossy and unwilling to share power and wealth." Each minority group believes it is discriminated against by a white-controlled society. But what they resent the most is that the white majority always sets the criteria and expects others to meet its standards, and that "integration" impacts most heavily on minorities.

Conclusion

To answer my colleague's charge that humanism is racist, I would have to give a qualified No.

Humanism is not inherently, intentionally, or overtly racist. However, there are some aspects of it that might make it appear so to minorities and oppressed people. There is evidence that we are not as advanced in becoming non-racist as we would like to think we are. There are things in our ideology, our language and our rigidity that place us behind the times in terms of the new directions the fight against racism is taking. We need to examine our precepts and language, and be open to hearing how they are experienced and perceived by minorities. We then have some important anti-racism work to do before we can begin to be active players in the next social movement of multiculturalism.

The goal of multiculturalism is to form a society in which all groups—racial, ethnic, national—can be fully and equally a part of the society, without having to give up their unique characteristics and identities. Ideally, it should be a society in which control and decision-making are shared equally, with no single group setting the standards. It would affirm the worth and dignity and difference of each member group, as well as each member of each group. But multiculturalism cannot become a reality until we have first conquered racism, oppression, and hate. These are the areas where humanism needs to muster its resources and place its energy now.

A truly multicultural society is probably a long way off. What we have now is several polyglot societies, with many different groups pulling away from the center, trying to maintain their identities, jostling for power and prestige, and fighting for recognition and acceptance. To reach the ideal of a multi-colored, multi-lingual, multi-cultured society where every group has equal status, yet each group maintains its own language and culture belonging to the larger society, is going to be very difficult. But this is the goal I believe humanists should strive to reach. It is time to recognize the deficiencies in some of our hallowed principles, and work along with others to build a truly multicultural society.

Notes

1. *Humanist Manifesto II*, 11th Article.

2. Kenneth Phifer, *The Faith of a Humanist* (Boston: Unitarian Universalist Association, 1993).

3. American Humanist Association Tract, 1997.

4. "Positive Humanism: Ten Non-Sectarian Principles" (Humanist Community of San Jose, CA, 1993).

5. *Humanist Manifesto I*, 5th Article.

6. *Humanist Manifesto II*, 4th Article.

7. Paul. L. LaClair, "A Humanist Orthodoxy," Speech to Ethical Culture Society, 1996.

8. Paul Kurtz, "Humanist Manifesto 2000," *Free Inquiry* 19:4 (Fall, 1999), p. 10.

9. Richard Erhardt, "Reason, Intellectual Elitism, Race, Class and Sex," *First Days Record* (Feb, 1998).

10. Patricia Waugh, *Practicing Postmodernism, Reading Modernism* (London: Edward Arnold, 1992), p. 74.

11. Cornel West, *Race Matters* (Boston: Beacon Press, 1993), p. 13.

12. Ibid., p. 15.

13. Ibid.

14. Mari Matsuda, et al., *Words That Wound: Critical Race Theory, Assaultive Speech, and the First Amendment* (Boulder: Westview Press, 1993), p. 94.

15. Ibid., p. 83.

16. Ibid., p. 65.

4

MULTICULTURALISM AND ME

Vern L. Bullough

In thinking about this topic, I concluded that perhaps a unique way of dealing with the subject and its meaning is to give a personalized history of multiculturalism. Let me begin by pointing out that multiculturalism in today's academic world as well as in much of the media is a politically correct term. Unfortunately it is often more a slogan than a reality. I found as a dean in the late 1980s, when the concept of multiculturalism first appeared, all my social science faculty emphasized that their classes had always been multicultural and so there was no need for a change in their syllabi. The historians said they taught courses on China and India and in their American history courses always included a lecture on minorities and on immigrants, the sociologists held their theory was universal, the political scientists claimed they taught comparative government. My fellow dean in the humanities had much the same response from his faculty with the modern language believing that nothing could be more multicultural than teaching French or Italian to American college students while the Literature people who taught world or comparative literature argued they were pioneers in multiculturalism. The list could go on. In a sense, they were right, but it is not multiculturalism in the sense that I define it. Neither for that matter does pluralism equate with multiculturalism although it might be a step in that direction. The United States has long been a pluralistic society but it has not been a multicultural one. The key difference as I would define the term is not the presence of a variety of cultures and peoples, but sharing power and ideas with them as well as recognizing their unique contributions to present day society. This is just beginning to occur. But it did not just happen. It has resulted from civil right campaigns, court decisions, empowerment of minorities, and just plain hard ball politics.

The dominant voice in the USA in the past was a European (really British), English speaking, and Christian one. In many if not most areas of the country, this is still true. The difference today, however, is that individuals and peoples of a variety of cultures and life styles have moved into positions of power and leadership and have effectively challenged what might be called a WASP culture in which White Anglo Saxon Protestant males dominated. This challenge is not a new one, and the battle to achieve it in a sense has been a major, if somewhat ignored theme in nineteenth and twentieth century history. It begun with attempts of the original settlers to deal with the Indians, and it was joined by German and Irish immigrants early on, and continued by each succeeding wave of settlers on American shores. Some of the struggles ended in violence such as the attempts of African Americans first to be freed from slavery and then from segregation. But transitions are not easy either for the establishment or for the challengers, and as the impeachment proceedings against Clinton emphasized, there is still a reluctance on behalf of many to accept changes in ideology and in power. This requires some explanation.

The United States has been built upon immigrants whether they came early or late. Many came in the nineteenth century to gain land for farming and the interesting thing about a large number of such settlements established in the nineteenth century in the Mid west and West is that they were segregated or perhaps ghettoized might be a better term. Germans lived in one small town, Norwegians, Dutch, or what have you in another. Traditionally the most ethnically diverse and multicultural areas were the large cities in the United States but in spite of their diversity and their economic power, they were not the dominant voices in the United States which remained overwhelmingly rural until well into the twentieth century. But the large cities were pluralistic not multicultural and cities like New York, Chicago, Philadelphia, Boston, had neighborhoods or concentrations of different national or cultural groups throughout the city. This was natural and perhaps inevitable since the new immigrants wanted to have contact with people who spoke their language or had other factors in common. Detroit, Chicago, Pittsburgh, Buffalo, Cleveland, and other cities had large Polish concentrations. Italians had their sections in New York, in Boston, in Philadelphia, in Chicago, Buffalo, San Francisco, and elsewhere. The list could go on with Slovaks, Czechs, Hungarians, Serbs, Russians, Germans, Swedes, Norwegians, Jews, and others. The Germans who arrived early and kept coming have left their imprint by having more Americans with some trace of German ancestry than any other group. Their influence has been much less than it might have been since the animosities raised by World War I and World War II towards Germans made them much less willing to identify as Germans than other immigrant groups. While my early childhood, for example, was spent in a community in which many still spoke German, few of the children my age ever learned it and many tried to disassociate themselves form things German. The schools also stopped teaching it and although the Christmas tree remains as a symbol of their influence, this too was made essentially American.

But even though America was a pluralistic society, power was mainly held by the WASP culture, in business, in education, in government (although on the state level there were some breakthroughs), and there were all kinds of barriers to those not conforming to the dominant American ideal. In fact, there was a reluctance to accept people who were visibly different. Let me illustrate by mentioning my own family. I had five children, three of whom were adopted. My adopted children were euphemistically called special need children since they were not white and two of them were not infants when they were adopted. My adopted children were Korean, black and one with considerable black genes but light enough to pass as Egyptian or Jewish or Greek even though her hair is somewhat frizzy.I mention this because it made me very conscious of where we could live and could not live. We lived in Los Angeles mainly because it was a diverse city with considerable internal movement, and the ghettoization which existed in Chicago or New York or Buffalo or any of the older eastern cities were not so rigidly drawn and there was much more integration there than almost everywhere else. Only when most of our children had grown could we venture to places like Buffalo, but even there in the eighties, Buffalo, in spite of the diversity of its population, was not really a multicultural center. We turned down good jobs in the south and although we probably could have survived in a small college town in the Midwest or East, we still felt uneasy. When we traveled, we were always the object of attention, some of it hostile, some of it simply curious. In East Berlin, for example, a bicycle rider ran into a wall because we apparently made such a fascinating sight that he did not look where he was riding. Generally, when the children were small, the attention was not particularly hostile, but as they grew older it did become more unfriendly. The civil rights battle of the 1960s made life somewhat easier but when I moved to Buffalo in the early eighties some of the neighbors in my upper class neighborhood refused to have anything to do with us even though we only had one black child at home. Many of my colleagues and friends in Buffalo came from a diversity of ethnic and racial backgrounds, and most of them told stories about how they had broken barriers of one kind or another to arrive at the positions they had achieved.

Pluralism then is not multiculturalism. Many societies have been pluralistic including Germany before World War II with several different languages, different Christian religions, a large Jewish minority, but it was not multicultural. The same thing was true of United States in the first half of the twentieth century. Let me illustrate with a case study of Postville, a real town in Iowa, which in the fifties could be taken to represent typical rural America. It had been settled in the middle of the nineteenth century by German and Norwegian immigrants and it took several generations for those two to get along since each had their own churches (although they were almost all Lutheran). With a population of 1500 in the 1960s, it was a center of farming and meatpacking. Unfortunately the local meat packing plant closed in the 1980s, and the threat of the collapse of the town was averted when a group of Hasidic Jews from New York City area bought the deserted plant and converted it into a kosher slaughterhouse. Perhaps the first sign of change was the appearance of three dozen rabbis to supervise the slaughter of cows and chickens. They obviously came with families. Until this happened most of the people in the town had never known a Jewish person nor had the ghettoized Hasidic Jews ever really mingled with non Jews, or for that matter with non orthodox Jews in the New York ghetto from which they came.

One of the things that happened is that pluralism reached small town Iowa but not multiculturalism. The Jews were quickly pegged as snobby by the local folk since they wouldn't eat in the local pizza joint (it wasn't kosher), or greet their neighbors warmly (among the Lubavich sect to which they belonged, men don't shake hands with women and women don't shake hands with men.) They were thought odd because all the little boys had their hair long since by tradition it should not be cut until age three, and then they usually wore yarmulkes. The women for their part wore wigs, covering their natural hair as part of a modesty code. Moreover the Lubavich Jews came from New York City and had the manners of big city dwellers. But to complicate matters the booming meat packing business forced the plant to go on two shifts in order to kill 350 cows and 35,000 chickens a day. This brought a lot of job seekers who were Filipino, Latino, Vietnamese, Bosnian, Ukrainian, and other refugees and new immigrant groups arriving in this country in the 1980s or 1990s. Certainly Postville was changing. It even soon had a kosher restaurant but for the most part the separate communities remained separate except the children often played together because the schools served as a common meeting ground.[1]

In a sense, late-twentieth century Postville, is a microcosm of what happened to urban America earlier in the century except the current generation of migrants had it somewhat easier because of civil rights and similar legislation giving them greater opportunity for jobs and education. Earlier when new immigrant groups and religious groups appeared, there was not much cross over in cultural contacts. There was suspicion of other groups and there were ghettoized neighborhoods all over. I lived in Youngstown, Ohio, early in my academic career. It had a variety of races, cultures, and religions, the "melting pot of America" but actually it was not. One was born and lived in a Polish, Italian, Serbian, Welch, German, Jewish, Irish, Chinese, Negro or what have you kind of neighborhood. I remember a discussion with one of my students who told me that his family was the first Italian family to move into Boardman, a suburb into which they had moved three years before. The city was beginning to change from a pluralistic and prejudiced community to a multi cultural one but the struggle to do so was long and hard. I had a colleague, a woman sociologist, whose husband was a minister of a Hungarian Presbyterian Church who argued that there should never be a melting pot in America. She wanted our society to be pluralistic, but with each group keeping its own heritage and traditions. Her husband was in some trouble, however, because the younger people did not want their services in Hungarian and insisted on an English language one, and some had even moved out of the confines of the Hungarian community and married outside of the group, an action which bothered her.

I myself had an interesting experience which got me fired from the university, at least temporarily. The university (then a private one, although now a public one) was really controlled by the owners of the mills (all Protestant), and they had reluctantly given support to the university in the hope of keeping the children of their workers in the area instead of having them go away to school and not come back. They themselves never sent their children to the local university but to Ivy League or similar schools. Most of the students I taught had come to the university in order to get out of the mills. In 1958, the Republican establishment of Ohio put a Right to Work initiative on the ballot, the perceived purpose of which was to weaken the unions, especially in the mills and factory towns such as Youngstown. I was opposed to the initiative, and obviously was somewhat left of center of the establishment. The labor unions called a rally to set up a citizen's committee to fight right to work. For presiding chair of the citizen's committee, they recommended an activist Catholic priest, and proposed that three co chairs be appointed with him, and those chosen included a Jewish dentist, a Serbian lawyer, and me. The slate had been agreed upon by the union before the meeting but I didn't know about it. When I asked why I (very much younger than the rest) was put on it, the answer was that they needed a Protestant, and I was the only one they knew or trusted. I told them I was not a Protestant but (at that time) a Humanist Unitarian, and they said no matter, you are not Catholic, or Jewish or Orthodox. They also added a woman as treasurer, and a black minister as secretary. This was pluralism in the political arena. Labor won big, and United States Senator, John Bricker, who had been identified with the Right to Work law, lost. The Trustees of the University who had backed the law blamed me and my "ilk" for this and while they couldn't do anything about the defeat, they could take their anger out on me. They fired me in a fit of pique. Actually, I did not stay fired because organized Labor intervened and I was kept on, but I decided to leave anyway.

In a sense this coming together for a cause was the incipient beginnings of multiculturalism. I should add that individual members of one of the cultural minorities could probably always make it through the barriers to achieve significant success in the Anglo world, they often never quite belonged and many had to turn their backs on their traditions. In Chicago, where I lived in the early

1950s, there were areas which did not allow Jews to live, and much later areas where African-Americans were prohibited, and admission to many of the universities and colleges was by quotas, if they were admitted at all. The first real national breakthrough on the parochialism of higher education was the hordes of veterans brought on campus by the GI Bill (I was one). Not only did many universities bend their racist and sexist admission barriers, but in order to have teachers for the students, broke down some of the traditional hiring barriers.

Before this time, most minorities took what they could get. In New York City, City College, became an intellectual center, mainly because of the large number of Jewish students in the 1930s and into the 1940s who went there because they could not get into most other universities and colleges. Some of the prestigious universities began to hire Jewish faculty members in the 1940s but many would not. Again let me report a personal experience.

When I decided to go to graduate school, the Western graduate schools were just beginning to appear, although Berkeley had long had a program and the University of Washington had one dating from before the Second World War. My faculty sponsor advised me to go East. I sent for applications to a number of Eastern schools (anything east of the Mississippi was east to me) I applied to several schools, and I still remember the application form from Princeton which I never filled out because it emphasized it was a school for good Christian men. Princeton, in fact, did not hire its first Jewish faculty member until the late 1950s.

Eventually, I chose to go to the University of Chicago which had the most polyglot faculty of any university at the time and a very mixed student body. The university, however, was an island of tolerance and pluralism in a sea of bigotry and discrimination which had only begun to break down. Sometimes ignoring this bigotry was already beginning to pay off. For example, the University of Utah, which I attended as an undergraduate, started its medical school in the late 1940s. The dean of the medical school, although a former Christian missionary, knew how to build, and what he did was recruit Jewish faculty, who were denied positions at most medical schools. This enabled the university to get a much faster start than it would have done otherwise and to do so with several national award winners on its faculty.

Another factor in changing the way the United States though was the baby boom of 1940s, and the products of this began to enter the universities in 1959 in force. Many new young faculty were hired to fill the professor gap and the average age of faculty declined. Adding to change and coinciding with the drop in average age of population in United States was the Civil Rights movement and the demands for blacks to achieve basic civil rights which in spite of U.S. constitution they had long been denied. Change was in the air, and it hit the college campus with all sorts of radical activity and demands, and a sympathetic faculty to listen to them.

California State University, Northridge, where I was then teaching, was ethnically and racially and linguistically diverse, although blacks remained a small minority. But it still was not a multi cultural institution since the curriculum remained in essence the standard one. American history, depending on the whims of the professor, was taught sometimes as if minorities never existed in the United States, or if they did., they had no history. Much of this changed in the late 1960s. In the middle sixties, when the college populations reached their height, and I again found myself in the middle of the change. I was president of the faculty and chair of the Academic Senate. The campus revolutions, which had started a year or so earlier at Berkeley, were spreading rapidly, fueled by the civil rights drive and the anti Vietnam war movement. . Some measure of the trouble on the Northridge campus was the fact that the fact that the administration building was set on fire, and over the year hundreds of students were arrested. So intense was the struggle that during my year of being a campus power, I served under five presidents. One had resigned, one had a nervous break-down, another was forced to resign, another agreed to serve three months and resigned, and finally a new president arrived who then served for some twenty years. In a sense and for a time, I ran the university, and I remember once giving a news conference in which the media representatives filled a 200 seat auditorium. One of the things I was able to persuade one of the acting presidents to do was to appoint a negotiating committee to meet with African-American residents of the northern section of the city, and with student groups who had been agitating for greater and more visible presence of blacks not only as students but as faculty and in subject matter. The situation was tense, and I, good liberal that I was, was bodily tossed out of the library by a Black Panther who was giving support to his black brethren. The negotiating committee I chose sat down with the various communities and student groups which I also managed to influence, in part because I was advisor to many of the student groups, and in part because I had founded the Fair Housing Council movement in southern California and had a lot of contacts across cultural groups. Fortunately while they were doing this, San Francisco State blew sky high, and its acting president, Hayakawa, convinced that he needed to control the media, deliber-ately set out to attract the press by his actions, and speeches. Since he made much more interesting copy than I did, they went there. We were able to settle the problems on the campus without the glare of publicity while Hayakawa kept San Francisco in turmoil for two years. I should add that he also was elected to the United States Senate because of this and I sometimes regret that I chose to negotiate rather than seek publicity. One of the agreements on the Northridge Campus as well as elsewhere was the appearance of Ethnic studies and African-American studies, as well as a pledge to break down even more of the hiring barriers and actively recruit visible minorities, physically handicapped, and others previously neglected groups for positions at the university. This became much easier than it might have been since the federal Civil Rights and Affirmative Action legislation put the force of government behind such action.

But the sixties saw other changes, the growth of a second wave of feminism which opened whole new areas for women, and the campaign for rights of gays and lesbians, and for what was euphemistically called the "Other Americans." I must admit I was in the forefront of all of these, and early wrote a book which became a standard in many course in women's studies, and I campaigned early on for rights of gays and lesbians, and wrote the ACLU policy for Southern California which ultimately became the national policy. Universities and society in general would never be quite the same. Slowly multiculturalism became a goal. By the seventies the Federal government was giving strong encouragement through grants to universities for what would be called multicultural activities. Course syllabi were rewritten to give attention to previously neglected groups. Publishers of books and journals, seeing a market jumped at it with a plethora of titles and articles. The color and gender of university faculties changed and groups long suppressed or content to be on the fringe pushed to the fore. Undoubtedly there were a lot of mistakes made, and standards in some of the special courses were not particularly high. I worked hard as a dean to lessen some of the excesses that had taken place. Still, the ultimate result was the emergence of large numbers of professionals of almost every race and color as well as being female, gay, lesbian, and disabled who came of age in the 1990s, and who have made our country more truly multicultural, not only in urban areas, and not only in academia but in business, the arts, and elsewhere.

The change has sometimes been traumatic. Not all Americans agree. What multiculturalism challenges is the idea of the United States as a Christian society. Although some version of Christianity remains the dominant religion, neither the mainline Protestants nor the Roman Catholics have the control they once did and the power base itself is changing. Whatever one may think of the difficulties that President Clinton found himself in, he really established the first multicultural gender-mixed administration in our history. And part of the hostility to him is that he has not acted as a good Baptist should.

The changes really are quite radical in many ways but in other ways things remain the same. I have been on the Board of the ACLU of Southern California, probably the most powerful affiliate of the ACLU, off and on for thirty-five years, and the same thing that happened in the university happened on the Board of that organization with a wide variety of nationalities, races, and what have you coming in and taking power. Still, the basic policies of the ACLU remain although they have broadened their outlook somewhat in accommodating to the new elements in American society.

Postville has its troubles, and it has a long way to go to reach a multi cultural condition, but at least they realize we live in a multi cultural world. Not everybody is ready for it, and there is a strong reaction. I find it interesting and worthy of note that most of the Republicans on the House Judicial Committee who led the impeachment drive of Clinton came from rural areas, and that southerners are disproportionate since that remains the most rural and least multicultural region of all the country in spite of Atlanta or Charlotte or Birmingham. In a sense, Trent Lott (who ran a racist campaign in Mississippi, switching to the Republicans when he felt his values threatened by the Johnson push for blacks, and who still has strong ties with the old White Citizens Councils) is fighting to preserve the world he knew before multiculturalism emerged as such force. This in part is what the country is now debating.

Multiculturalism, however, is more than simply something American. In the long run, it is adopting what we are trying to do in the United States to a better understanding of what goes on in the rest of the world. While people everywhere are human, and many countries are pluralistic, multiculturalism is something that requires deliberate effort. It takes education, lobbying, understanding, and idealism. Multiculturalism, I think, is Humanism writ large. Our argument for tolerance, acceptance of diversity, and emphasis on what an individual can do, regardless of race, color, creed, sexual orientation, marital state, physical ability, and the like, is the key to multiculturalism. It has allowed individuals and groups who in the past have been relegated to positions beneath their abilities, to participate and achieve. I think it has been an interesting experience and I hope that we can continue in the direction we are going. It does not eliminate using the criteria of merit or ability, but it does say that merit and ability is not restricted to white males who graduated from Ivy League Colleges. We can continue living in our old neighborhoods if we want, but one does not have to become something he or she is not comfortable with; increasingly instead each person has an opportunity to contribute to society on their own merit. It also means we have to make a continual effort to break through our own parochialism and become more aware of the world around us. Hopefully, multiculturalism is here to stay although our society is still not fully accepting of the implications which real multiculturalism might bring about. We just might end up with a new version of a pluralistic society with strong multiculturalist element.

Note

1. My description of Postville is based on a *Los Angeles Times* story, January 26, 1999, pp. A1, A8.

5

LIBERALISM, PLURALISM, AND MULTICULTURALISM IN THE TWENTY-FIRST CENTURY

Michael Werner

The Problem

Our problem is to cast light and direction on the humanist agendas for the twenty-first century regarding the issues of pluralism, liberalism, and multiculturalism; three words in ascending order of historical origin that serve as viewpieces for understanding humanism as the century passes into a new era. Is there a future for liberalism? What is our reading of the criticisms of humanism and liberalism by multiculturalists? In a smaller world where cultures, religions, and races freely intersperse to form more diverse societies, what form of multicultural society is most desirable? Are we to be, pluralist or assimilationists, i.e. the salad bowl or the soup bowl? How are minorities to be protected in this fast changing, largely uncontrolled process?

Background

Liberalism

Liberalism has been an evolving pattern of ideas and traditions rising primarily out of the Western cultures. Fed by the ancient Greeks' use of reason, the Germanic tribes' passion for freedom, the Roman development of law, and the anticlerical sentiment of the Renaissance, liberalism clarified much of its vision by the time of the Enlightenment. David Gress[1] sees Western liberalism as resting on a three-legged stool of reason, democracy and freedom. Classic liberalism has been, until recently, the tradition that has "fought against religious intolerance, intellectual obscurantism, confining traditions, and obsequious forms of dependence." "Pluralism, freedom, rights, equality and distributive justice are the basic values of liberalism," according to John Kekes:

> Essential to liberalism is the moral criticism of dictatorship, arbitrary power, intolerance, repression, persecution, lawlessness, and the suppression of individuals by entrenched orthodoxies. Reason and morality are on the side of the liberals and against their opponents in this moral criticism .[2]

Isaiah Berlin's famous essay "Two Concepts of Liberty"[3] analyzes liberalism's debate concerning freedom. Negative freedom looks at external restrictions to liberty and asks the question, "Who is the master?" Positive freedom focuses on the results in our lives towards gaining freedom and asks, "How far am I the master?" Berlin rejected the activist notions of positive freedom as part of liberalism's agenda because it leads to totalitarianism. Other thinkers, such as Marxists, have thought that cultural transformation by positive freedom should be the prime cause of liberalism. Liberalism up to this century had been fairly unified, but the schism in theory and practice, just described, has left classical liberalism, as it enters the twenty-first century, in a quandary as to what its overall agendas should be, especially regarding the political arena.

Pluralism

Pluralism is the belief that there are many reasonable ways of living a good life. It promises that people should be able to choose freely among all the available alternatives. It is in contrast to a monist view of life that there is only one proper [Read as rational?] way to live our lives. A monist presupposes a universal civilization is desirable, needed, and possible. Isaiah Berlin, popularized, but did not invent, the notion of pluralism. He sees a

> value-pluralism, that ultimate human values are objective but irreducibly diverse, that they are conflicting and often uncombinable, and when they do come into conflict with one another they are incommensurable; that is, they are not comparable by any rational measure.[4]

Further,

> The idea of a perfect society in which all genuine ideals and goods are achieved is not merely utopian; it is incoherent. Political life, like moral life, abounds in radical choice between rival goods and evils, where reason leaves us in the lurch and whatever is done involves loss and sometimes tragedy. Berlin's is a tragic liberalism of unavoidable conflict and irreparable loss among inherently rivalrous values.

John Gray[5] goes even further arguing that there are no philosophical foundations for liberalism and sees liberalism and pluralism in deep conflict. His is a relativistic/postmodern pluralism where there are no privileged or better forms of living that we should "accord a central place in human life." This is a pluralism of radical egalitarianism as it holds that pluralism may sanction non-liberal or even illiberal cultures.

On the other hand, John Kekes, a conservative philosopher, argues for traditional liberal pluralism saying that

> whatever is worth saving from liberalism is contained in a version of pluralism, which is the best candidate for an acceptable political morality. This version of pluralism, however, is not a form of mitigated relativism. It is committed to the protection of the conditions that good lives require regardless of how they are conceived, provided that they are within the bounds of reason. [6]

He argues that overall, liberalism is inadequate, irrational and inconsistent because there is no sufficient theory for evil. The liberal high value of radical pluralism and egalitarianism (even Berlin's version) do not necessarily lead to the good society because they do not confront the evilness that some societies and cultures inculcate.

Other observers, such as Ronald Dworkin, Thomas Nagel, and John Rawls see no conflict between liberalism and pluralism, but obviously the rent in the liberal fabric is too wide today to ignore.

Multiculturalism

Popular notions of multiculturalism are as much bound in demographic and political realities as they have to do with ideology. The mobility of interspersing cultures and the globalization of mass media has meant that no culture is isolated. I had this idea indelibly thrust on me some years ago when I saw a family, in a hut with a dirt floor, in the Ecuadorian Amazon jungle watching "Dynasty" on TV. More recently I noted that about half of my neighbors are not White Anglo-Saxon.

I distinguish here the difference between the academic definition of multiculturalism and the more popular usage which is more concerned with the practical problems/opportunities of dealing with a multicultural society. For many, living in a multicultural society means the joy of having a great dinner at a Thai restaurant, or dealing with the concern that more and more of your neighbors don't look or act like you. Most people can appreciate other cultures, but have real problems with having another culture be the dominant one over their own. America has never been multicultural, but has been assimilationist. In America, we may talk about the "salad bowl" but what we really want is the hot fires of the "melting pot" and we are no different than any other culture in this regard. A totalitarianism of the majority always seems to dominate.

As an academic ideology, multiculturalism has taken the lead from Gray's analysis of pluralism and other postmodernist theorists and argue that Western civilization is in fact oppressive, anti-humanistic and that other cultures offer better or least equal options. They argue that there is no culture superior to any other and we should revel in the culture of our choice, while affirming all other possibilities as equally valid.

The Critique of Western Humanistic Civilization

The critique of Western civilization and the liberal humanist/modernist project in particular, has come from many sources. Max Weber[7] originally saw religion, economics, and culture intimately mixed so that our secular religion is really consumerism and capitalism. He extended the earlier Marxist theory that the economic system predicates the culture, religion, morals, etc. and not the other way around. Later, the Frankfurt School produced a group of Marxist philosophers trying to rethink socialism in light of the Stalinist purges. Out of this school grew the classic influential book, *Dialectic of the Enlightenment,* by Max Horkheimer and Theodor Adorno[8] that saw freedom, reason, and individual authenticity as tools of a capitalist culture to promote and keep vested classes in power rather than the liberating ideals that classic liberalism saw in them. Many see their attempt to destroy ideas of freedom, reason and individual authenticity as merely a rationalization to justify Marxist totalitarianism.

The 1960s counterculture movement welcomed a neo-Romanticism that repudiated reason and science and celebrated the subjective self. Some feminists criticized reason as a tool of men to rationalize power and control,[9] Some environmentalist saw technology as science's handmaiden and destroying the earth.[10] By placing humans at the top of our values, David Ehrenfield says, we have raped the environment for our own good.

Underclasses, especially African Americans, saw education as a "white thing" to keep them oppressed. Reason, science and education in general are great, some argued, but they are only available in reality to rich, white, males in the suburbs. The argument for lifting yourself by your boot straps only applies if you have boots. Today's boots to advance oneself are education, culture, and money and are unequally available. Blacks, Hispanics, and women, especially in the inner city, don't really have access to these tools.

Some multiculturalists have argued that nonscientific "primitive" cultures, such as the early Native Americans, lead or have led more decent lives than so-called "civilized culture" with its disintegrating social fabric, oppression, and poverty. The idea of a humanist culture, so the argument goes, is a pretense at its heart for subjugating minorities and minority cultures.

What Do We Do?

Space does not permit a detailed rebuttal of the critiques of Western civilization. I take great issue with many of the modernist critiques, but also find important truths imbedded in the knots of madness. Sometimes it takes extremism to uncover hidden problems. Still, its difficult to unravel the truth from the interconnecting knots of a millennium madness that suffocates our minds in the dense fog of obscurantism, diversionary political issues, tortured logic and language. These are webs that ultimately bind our heart to only the most superficial of commitments.

It seems to me one of the most important questions we can ask is whether there are transcultural values, i.e. those that transcend culture, time, ethnicity, sex, race, and all the other criteria of difference. Secondly, and possibly the more important question, is whether those values make a difference or even have any chance of being incorporated into a common global culture. Human universals come from the twin aspects of nature and necessity. Our empirical, scientific data base provides a sounder footing than the rarified air of philosophy where universal rights and Platonic ideals dominate. Some of the necessary transcultural realities are survival (which includes food, clothing, shelter and protection), the realities of a social world (it's harder and harder to be hermit today), and our necessary dependence on our genes.

During much of this century, there has been a rejection, or at least a diminishment of the importance of a universal nature.[11] John Locke's concept of a "blank slate" rejected any theory of human nature. More recently, the nature/nurture controversy pendulum has swung back to an acknowledgment that our genes provide important limitations and drives to our behavior. We are only beginning to tease out the roots of our motivations in the tangle of our genetic and cultural drives.

Anthropologists have found hundreds of transcultural traits. Donald E. Brown studied thousands of cultures and found that many patterns of behavior can be assembled to describe a "Universal People."[12] Universal is a strong word here, but signifies that these traits are found in almost or all cultures in crosscultural studies. The universals range from empathy, division of labor, fear of snakes, hygiene, laws, rights, rituals including rights of passage, deploring of conflict, a sense of right and wrong, status and prestige, male dominance in politics, dance, woman's dominant role in child care, smiling to indicate friendliness, supernatural beliefs, magic, and a sense of fairness among many others.

Some would argue that certain liberal, western oriented traits such as freedom, reason, science, democracy, education, free market economy, and equal worth and dignity are inherent in the human condition and are winning over in other cultures where they were either already present or suppressed and just now rising. It does appear that classical liberalism is being confirmed in many cultures and not just by Western hegemony. This is not to say that there are not many functionally viable alternatives for leading a happy life. This is also not to say that all people will or even should agree with Western Enlightenment principles. Most important, classical liberalism sees a society that is not totally monocultural; i.e., It is one in which there are always some radical departures from the cultural norm, and provides healthy communities in self-reflective pluralistic dynamic.

Still, as Robert Hughes and others have noted, "American ideas of liberal democracy are only to be nourished at their sources, which lie absolutely within the European tradition."[13] Moreover, William Henry in his book *In Defense of Elitism* says:

Education is elitist. Civilization is elitist. Egalitarianism celebrates the blissful ignorance of the Garden of Eden, where there were no Newtons to perceive the constructive use of the apple. The point of elitism is not, when all is said and done, to promote envy or to enlarge their numbers of society's losers. It is to provide sufficient rewards for winning, and sufficient support for ideas that shaped past progress and that might aid future progress so that society as a whole wins—that is, gets richer, better educated, more productive, and healthier.[14]

While I sympathize with Berlin's liberalism, I think he goes too far at times with his concept of pluralism. His concept of liberalism being "tragic" in that we will always have unavoidable conflicts is one of the twentieth century's most simple but profound insights. Still, he saw no rational reason for universal goals and methods. I think he lacked an understanding of the scientific basis for human nature. The nature/necessity argument I have presented gives us a rational basis for that universality that he sought, but did not find. Norman Podhoretz, a conservative writing about Berlin's pluralism says,

> We see this…(lack of courage)…once again today in the supine response of liberals to "multiculturalism," which can be understood as a diseased mutation of the pluralism that Isaiah Berlin never ceased extolling. As Berlin expounded it had a real force when fascism and Communism were riding high, and when, to its eternal honor, it formed one of the crucial elements making the case for bourgeois democracy as the superior alternative. But today, when "multiculturalism" is all the rage, in England as well as in America, it can be of no help and may even do harm in the struggle to prevent the balkanization of our common culture and the dissolution of our common intellectual and academic standards.[15]

The mutation he speaks of certainly applies to the excessive postmodern, multicultural, relativistic ideas represented by John Gray.

I think that one must consider whether liberalism will out in the Darwinian battle of the alternatives and what we might do about it. No one knows what the future globalized world will look like. What we should do, it seems, is to prepare for the varying alternatives. We might actually be moving towards a humanist dominated monoculture. Then again, I think it is just as likely that we might see a future where our Enlightenment values are only used selectively by a diverse amalgam of isolated cultures. We might end up being minorities having to contend with antihumanistic cultures in pluralistic flux. Our practical strategies for dealing with all the strange realities we might encounter should then take precedence over tilting at windmills in a world not to our liking.

Liberal Values under Siege

Francis Fukuyama in his book *The End of History and the Last Man*[16] proposes that science, democracy and capitalism are dominating the world scene regardless of any perceived temporary deviations. We are moving with historical inevitability towards a Western monoculture strictly by the inherent force of these tools. Conversely, Patrick Kennon in his book *The Twilight of Democracy*[17] argues that democracy, one of the bulwarks of liberalism, is actually dying worldwide. History has shown that as soon as countries achieve democracy, they soon begin to ignore it and power elites take over and generally run the country. The Eastern communist countries who fought so hard for the freedom of the ballot box came out in 90 percent voting percentages in the first elections. Thereafter their numbers settled into those that resemble the United States at around 25 percent. Also, he notes that rather than through democracy, it is only through more authoritarian systems that underdeveloped countries advance to a point where they then have the education, civilization, and social stability to handle and sustain a democracy.

Regarding capitalism, the future landscape is even murkier. None less than the most prominent capitalist thinker of this century, Peter Drucker, has proclaimed that both capitalism and socialism are dead and that we are in a new era he terms "Post-Capitalism."[18] We have no theory for this brave new world of information age, global economy, and are entering an era without understanding, direction, vision, or control. One thing is clear: the old theories and categories no longer work.

Fukuyama sees science as a progressive harmonizing world force. Others, such as Carl Sagan, have noted that while we are benefactors of science and technology, we are becoming increasing scientific illiterates. At best, most people use reason and science selectively. The situation may be even more exacerbated in the future. John Horgan in his book *The End of Science*[19] points to the inherent limitations of *basic* scientific knowledge. In many cases, such as my own field of chemistry, where no major new theory has been discovered since the 1930s, we are merely filling in the decimal points, as they say. Other fields, such as physics, may be hitting up against either an economic wall or against inherent limitations to our understanding. There are, of course, always blossoming areas of new discovery such as cognitive neuroscience, but we may be entering a twenty-first century where science is not the burgeoning and exciting field in the public's eye that the twentieth century was. We may see the quality of science students decline in the future simply because it will be harder to make rewarding discoveries. A physicist at Fermi lab told me that physics is not attracting the overall general genius that it once did, but more the specialists who can only do physics. This comment came after speaking with Leo Lederman, the past head of Fermi lab, who someone said would probably have been a stand up comedian if he had not been a scientist. Will the future defenders of science be fewer in number, authority, and public prestige? Will the best and brightest be drawn to entertainment and Wall Street? Will we all be users of science's power without knowing how science works? An illiterate tribesman can pull the trigger on a nuclear device. Last year in the United States, 60 percent of the population did not read a book.

Lastly, the Kantian/Christian notion of acknowledging equal dignity, respect, and worth for each individual shows fraying at the edges of both theory and practice. This bulwark of humanist sentiment is challenged in Peter Singer's book *Rethinking Life and Death*[20] in which he asks us to consider where concepts of variable worth and dignity are appropriate. It is uncharted and dangerous intellectual land for humanists.

What Future for Liberal Culture?

My sense is that the future world will tend more towards disarray than order, fragmentation rather than coherence. We are likely to see a combination of radical individualism, tribalism, regionalism, and globalism tugging at our social fabric. Samuel Huntington in his book *The Clash of Civilizations and the Remaking of the World Order*[21] has introduced us to the idea of a reactionary future world with globalization. He sees the result being the balkanization and conflict of various cultures primarily along cultural/religious lines. Samuel Huntington says,

> Multiculturalism at home threatens the United States and the West; universalism abroad threatens the West and the world. Both deny the uniqueness of Western culture. The global monoculturalists want to make the world like America. The domestic multiculturalists want to make America like the world. A multicultural America is impossible because a non-Western

America is not American. A multicultural world is unavoidable because a global empire is impossible. The preservation of the United States and the West requires the renewal of Western identity. The security of the world requires acceptance of global multiculturality.[22]

Contrary to popular thinking, recent studies have shown that America is much more monolithic in culture than previously supposed.[23] The melting pot still boils.

Western values of freedom, science, reason, free market economy, individual worth etc. will need whole new interpretations. Liberals in this century had reason to believe that the universalistic effects of the grand narrative of humanism/modernism would lead to a global monoculture—many still believe this. I am much more skeptical. Even Francis Fukuyama now admits that totalitarianism or anarchism may ultimately win over democracy. Robert Hughes fears "A Hobbesian world: the war of all on all, locked in blood-feud and theocratic hatred, the *reductio ad insanitatem* of America's mild and milky multiculturalism." Many predict a world dominated by global media/business if that has not already happened. David Gress notes that,

> Universalists argue that the West needs to discard its historical identity to accommodate other cultures; in effect they argue that the fate of the West is to be multicultural. Nothing could be further from the truth. A multicultural West is a contradiction in terms; the only West that can be accommodating to other cultures is a West that knows itself and, on the strength of that understanding, encounters other cultures. An empty vessel, a historically illiterate people cannot give to others the respect it does not give itself.[24]

I totally agree. Our pragmatic approach should be to encourage a new humanism as Gress says, where "the triad of reason, liberty and prosperity which remains the unavoidable and indeed valuable framework of the New West, not be distorted into rationalism, license and self-gratification."[25] All of our greatest humanist ideals of reason, science, progress, freedom, and inherent individual worth have limitations, problems and the lies of simplicity about them as I have argued here. Our future task is to encourage a reformulation of these ideals and then speak to a future audience, possibly hostile and threatened by our Western values, but where these ideals can have the practical effect of enhancing their lives. We must speak to people that suffer inherited disadvantages especially in education and culture: cultures where as Cornel West says there is, "too much poverty and too little self love."[26] Abandoning reason and science because they are tools of power elites in the oppression of minorities is not the answer, for as Noam Chomsky points out, then only the power elites will have these tools. He also asks, "What is the alternative to reason?"

We have seen a number of excesses regarding liberalism's basic foundations that, while instructive, have served to undermine unifying, core, transcultural principles in the service of global welfare. We have no need to apologize for humanist principals. Standing up for these principles also means standing up for honest, rational, or even irrational pluralistic differences. There is a balancing act required of us to value differences while not slipping into a relativistic multiculturalism devoid of a moral center. It is in an adaptable, humbler, tolerant, yet still confident humanism that real gains can be made for future human and global welfare.

Notes

1. David Gress, *From Plato to NATO* (New York: Free Press, 1998), p. 213.

2. John Kekes, *Against Liberalism* (Ithaca, NY: Cornell University Press, 1997), p. 212.

3. Isaiah Berlin, *Four Essays on Liberty, Two Concepts of Liberty* (London: Oxford University Press, 1969).

4. John Gray, *Isaiah Berlin* (Princeton, NJ: Princeton University, 1996), p. 1.

5. John Gray, *Liberalisms* (London: Routledge, 1989).

6. John Kekes, *Against Liberalism,* p. 212.

7. Max Weber, *Economy and Society* (Berkeley CA: University of California Press, 1909).

8. Max Horkheimer and Theodor W. Adorno, *Dialectic of Enlightenment* (New York: Continuum, 1944).

9. Ann Garry and Marilyn Pearsall, *Woman's Way of Knowing* (Boston: Allen Unwin, 1989).

10. David Ehrenfield, *The Arrogance of Humanism* (Oxford: Oxford University Press, 1978), p. 1.

11. Carl N. Degler, *In Search of Human Nature* (New York: Oxford Press, 1991).

12. Donald E. Brown, *Human Universals* (New York: McGraw Hill, 1991).

13. Robert Hughes, *Culture of Complaint* (New York: Oxford University Press, 1993).

14. William A. Henry, *In Defense of Elitism* (New York: Doubleday, 1994), pp. 26, 59.

15. Norman Podhoretz, "A Dissent on Isaiah Berlin," *Commentary* (February 1999), p. 37.

16. Francis Fukuyama, *The End of History and the Last Man* (New York: Free Press, 1992).

17. Patrick Kennon, *The Twilight of Democracy* (New York: Doubleday, 1995), intro.

18. Peter Drucker, *Post-Capitalist Society* (New York: Harper, 1993), intro.

19. John Horgan, *The End of Science* (Reading, MA: Addison-Wesley, 1996).

20. Peter Singer, *Rethinking Life and Death* (New York, St. Martin's Press, 1994), p. 202.

21. Samuel P. Huntington, *The Clash of Civilizations and the Remaking of World Order* (New York: Simon & Schuster, 1996).

22. Ibid., p. 318.

23. Alan Wolfe, *One Nation After All* (New York, Viking, 1998).

24. Ibid., p. 556.

25. Ibid., p. 559.

26. Cornel West, *Race Matters* (Boston, MA: Beacon, 1993) p. 63.

6

EVOLUTIONARY PRINCIPLES OF ADAPTATION

IMPLICATIONS FOR MULTICULTURALISM

Philip J. Regal

Introduction

Evolutionary biology, at its best, is a science that deals with principles of the survival, adaptation, and patterns of change of organic life, as well as with philosophical questions about whether there is progress or "improvement" in nature. It seeks as well to understand the causes of failures of populations to adapt to local conditions and of the extinctions of entire species.

Evolutionary perspectives should be considered when contemplating issues that have been raised with regard to multiculturalism. In brief, evolutionary principles offer reasons to be optimistic about the possibilities that respect for multiculturalism offers our species. On the other hand, multiculturalism is too often seen to be a major practical and philosophical problem from perspectives that have long dominated philosophical discourse in Western civilization.

Plato's response to the practical problems that were presented by the cultural diversity among Greeks was to argue for a single model of ontological reality and social practice, as though this would have ended discord and insured the future enlightenment of Greek peoples. If one thinks the proposition through closely, though, it seems doubtful that this approach, however superficially seductive and appealing, could bring true peace in the long run or could allow full exploration of the human creative potential. Conflicts of material interest would arise, there would be struggles between individuals to rule and to benefit from holding positions of power, and the human spirit might well in the end reject any system that did not leave room for a diversity of individual and community perspectives.

In any event, when Idealistic perspectives on what the human condition should be began long ago, they were formulated without any appreciation for the processes that have generated the diversity of life on earth. The Idealistic tradition has continued into our own time despite its failures, but with such historical force behind it that intellectuals too often simply debate the alternative Idealisms that have been and are being pursued without stopping to consider that it could be useful to begin to consider that fresh intellectual approaches are possible.

This essay will begin by considering the powerful Idealistic forces that struggle today to promote their visions for future society. It will conclude by making the point that the diversities and their mixing and remixing—viewed by those diversities these Idealisms may treat as "noise in the system" or as preludes to chaos—can from another more modern scientific perspective be thought of as valuable assets that can keep humanity equipped to remain in the game of adaptation and improvement that has insured the survival and diversification of life on the planet.

Four Idealistic Horsemen Race
to Control Humanity's Future

What factions might well become the Philosopher Kings of the future? Whose ideas of Truth and Rationality might well become the orthodox patois of social discourse?

The would-be Guardians and Philosopher Kings who struggle for power face a planet and a humanity that is in fact culturally and intellectually diverse. What does this imply from their philosophical perspectives? It is not too serious a caricature to say that they all see the diversity of the world as largely chaotic insofar as it exists beyond their control. It is the chaotic, irrational Receptacle that requires the Demiurge to impose the Good, Reason, and order upon it.

In the real world, concentrations of power over society have typically been possible because of alliances, often seemingly improbable alliances, and this will probably be true in the struggles for power over the future of humanity. But for the purposes of scholarly analysis, it is useful to survey some of the leading competitors who race to become the Guardians of world society in the twenty-first century as though they are independent actors in the scramble for power. What ideas and terms of discourse identify the major factions who have been lobbying politicians and administrators at all levels with enormous effectiveness, who have been filling important government and industry positions with sympathetic minds, who have been working effectively for laws and courts and media story-lines that will favor their causes?

Economic Guardians

The greatest collection of interests that has vast power today, and that seeks to extend its enormous power to even greater heights in the future, rallies around and promotes the so-called free-market ideology that was developed by Bernard Mandeville in the early eighteenth century, that was refined and elaborated by by Adam Smith in the late eighteenth century, and made into virtually a complete cosmology by Herbert Spencer in the mid nineteenth century. The social landscape that these neo-liberals map it is economic, and their economic language and rituals of economic reasoning are Rationality for them. The in-groups that have intellectual respectability within this set of interests are legitimate in their eyes by virtue of philosophy and reason, while the out-groups are irrational and have no natural right to make decisions for society.[1]

Philosophical economics tends only to embrace cultural and intellectual diversity that fits in with its Idealistic schemes—market-fostering diversity, for example. The economic system needs sets of producers and consumers, management and labor, diverse types of training, richly rewarded life-styles as models for motivation juxtaposed against pools of cheap labor. Otherwise, cultural diversities can appear to be manifestations of chaos that threaten the stability of the system. Thus environmentalisms, commune-isms, non-materialistic and independent religious and philosophical movements amount to threats that must, if they become too great, be either crushed or else co-opted and made part of the world machine. The ethic is "survival of the productive" as defined in economic terms. The rest must be sloughed off, one way or another.

Molecular Guardians

A fast-advancing set of interests in the struggle to be the Philosopher Kings of the twenty-first century is the growing community of molecular biologists and genetic engineers and the lawyers and other non-scientists who have joined this profit venture. The modern roots of their reductionistic and deterministic world-views trace back to the dreams of the Natural Theologians, Descartes, and Newton. Reductionism and determinism and the idealisms in which these have been wrapped are the True Realities and molecule-speak is Rationalism. Others are irrational and have no natural right to make decisions for society. They must be brought into the fold or be left to go extinct.[2]

The reductionist and genetic determinist core of molecular biology and genetic engineering has labeled small tribal cultures "artifacts of historical interest" and similarly the ideology only values non-human biological diversity for its "genetic gold." Life is a code to be cracked, patented, engineered, and brought under the control of the new scientific elite and their allies. The imperfections of organic and cultural nature will be left behind in the jet stream of history as its chemical research and industrial power carries humanity and nature both into a utopian future. Life is something that can only be understood properly by those who have been indoctrinated into molecular chemistry and the philosophical doctrines on which it rests. Sociobiologists may also be admitted into the ranks of this biological elite so long as they are loyal to the Grand Agenda of the philosophical reduction of human behavior to the arrangements of bits of DNA without any serious need to consider emergent properties, the vagaries of cultural history, or the independent agency of human imagination in the long view of human societies and values.[3]

A third force with long-standing political savvy and clout in the struggles for power is the hierarchy of the Roman Catholic Church, with its long familiar doctrines and political perspectives.

Guardians of the Body of Christ on Earth

The Roman Catholic world-view is patient, but ambitious. It is human destiny that one day all humanity will become well-organized parts of the Body of Christ on earth. The parts of the body will follow directions established by the Vicar of Christ. The popes and cardinals will be the ultimate Guardians, because their vision for humanity will be based not only on tradition and theological study, but on inspiration from God.

The Guardians of Social Conservativism

A fourth force has been formed by diverse types of evangelical Protestants in the English-speaking world. They have been taught great political, organizational, and marketing skills from their political allies in business and the military and they have gained great political clout. Despite their sociological diversity and their diversity with regard to complex theological issues, they have managed to forge an ideology that holds them together and that would serve as a template for Rational thought where they can take power. Their ideology depends in part on sharable hatreds and theories about the nature of evil in the world. They have constructed a shared theory about so-called liberalism (actually American centrism combined with the left, not to be confused with the economic neo-liberals above) that contends that so-called liberalism is the cause of all that is wrong in society it must be torn down in a "culture war." Again, they are uncompromising and those who disagree with them are dupes and have no divinely sanctioned or natural right to take part in social decisions.

Evangelical fundamentalist worldviews are diverse, but most tend to be charismatic, and their beliefs commonly contain versions of Persian dualisms. There is Evil and it is their obligation to fight Evil vigorously. Their leaders have formed political alliances with the capitalists and even Roman Catholics, and these fundamentalists (a better term may be "literalists") have been persuaded that "the liberals" who supposedly caused the modern age, with all its disorder and sin are their natural enemies. Their goal has been to destroy culture and thinking that that is alien to them. They are horrified by "multiculturalism," "sexual diversity," "women's liberation." Many of them further are offended by scientific perspectives that question the biblical versions of Creation, or the idea that fertilized eggs may not have souls and a clear destiny to become fully human.[4]

Minor Contenders

Buddhism, Hinduism, Islam and state communism in their absolutist versions cannot be entirely discounted, but they do not seem well poised to form decisive ideological alliances with the most organized and best funded contenders for power that have been mentioned. This could change, but at present they lack the organizational skills, determination, and other ingredients that would identify them as serious contenders. This is a complex matter, however. China, for example has been experimenting with ideological and practical alliances between state communism and "market capitalism."

The Irrationality of Idealisms:
An Evolutionary Biological Perspective

Evolutionary biology, non-Spencerian evolutionary biology that is, offers a perspective on cultural diversity that contrasts to the idealisms of today's power seekers and their ideologies. A scientific understanding of the mechanisms of natural selection implies that a diversity of organic, functional, traits is essential to adaptive dynamics and to the long-term survival of species.

Genetics is more than DNA. It is DNA arranged into dynamic systems that continually scramble and reorganize biochemical information and test new combinations of traits in the arena of survival and reproduction. DNA is arranged in ways that make it create novelty within the sex cells, and plants and animals behave in nature so as to combine DNA in still more novel ways. The generation of diversity has been the key to the survival and evolution of species.

Sex cells, for example, are produced by a meiotic process that carefully scrambles a significant fraction of the genetically determined traits of each individual. Then sexual intercourse combines this scrambled genetic information with the scrambled genetics of a second individual to produce novel offspring. The generation of novelty in this way has the important function of providing raw materials for improved modes of adaptation to the environment and in terms of the improved internal organization of morphology and physiology. It also provides the raw materials for new adaptative modes in the event that environmental conditions change. Similarly, while there are parts of the DNA code that are protected from mutation by effective molecular repair mechanisms, other parts have been left open to the production of genetic diversity by mutation.

There are chemical and behavioral mechanisms to limit inbreeding and to promote outbreeding, which generates further genetic variability at the level of the population and of neighboring populations.

Genetic differences between multiple populations over a small or large landscape have been found to be important sources of genetic variability and sites for "experimentation" with novel genetic combinations. Natural selection "works out," so to speak, balances between diverse traits and arranges them into sets. Then there are mechanisms to insure dispersal between populations, and diverse sets of traits thus come together and combinations of sets of sets are in turn subjected to tests of natural selection.

Evolutionary studies suggest that while it may be possible for the variability "dial" to be "set" too high such that mutation, outbreeding, etc. would generate excessive novelty, the generation of an enormous amount of genetic diversity has become normal in microorganisms, plants, and animals because it has been advantageous for adaptation and survival.

Selfing and parthenogenetic species, in which there is very little new genetic diversity, can have strong competitive ecological advantages in some situations. They can even wipe out competitors in some cases. One might say that these are "rational adaptive strategies," but only in very particular ecological conditions, and only for the limited time periods when given ecological conditions prevail. For example, selfing species rapidly colonize disturbed areas. But the evidence is that selfing and parthenogenesis have held very little evolutionary "promise" in the long run and thus they are considered to be evolutionary blind alleys.

Spencerian or social Darwinist logic will argue that, to the contrary, organic diversity must be pruned away, and that competition and defeat of the weak are the key to adaptation and evolution. In this over-simplified view, it would actually be the reduction of diversity that is key to adaptation and evolution, not the generation and preservation of diversity.

This Spencerian argument is in fact an Idealism. It is a half-truth that was invented to give pictorial persuasiveness to Spencer's so-called free-market and cultural progressivist ideologies. The Spencerian half-truth is seriously misleading. The fact is that the majority of DNA in sexual organisms has been arranged by eons of evolution into forms (recessive states) and configurations on chromosomes (linkage groups) that protect much of the genetic variation in nature and hide it from being quickly extinguished by natural selection. It is as though evolution has treated genetic novelty as a precious thing even if a given novelty has low value to the organism at any specific time.

Novel DNA of small value ("low fitness") is protected on chromosomes by being located alongside older bits of DNA (i.e. in linkage groups) that have established high fitness values. Moreover, novel bits of DNA commonly are hidden in "recessive" states that only express and become fully visible to natural selection occasionally, under unusual circumstances (homozygous conditions, and genetic and environmental conditions that increase "penetrance," i.e. expression) and thus recessive DNA can spread and recombine "silently." Recessive DNA is very difficult to remove by natural selection.

One would have to conclude that if there were indeed a Grand Designer, the Designer's strategy was to to make sure that genetic novelties that had any hint of value (that were not immediately lethal) would not be eliminated until endless combinations of such novelties had been tested for endless circumstances in which they might be valuable in the real world.

I am reminded of the Hollywood film studio lots where I worked my way through college. There were huge warehouses filled with old automobiles, clothing, furniture, oddities. There were great film vaults filled with stock footage of a rich variety of events and scenes. Experience had taught the film community that this was prudent management even in purely economic terms, for one never knew when something quite old or quite odd would be needed for a future production that might become a box office hit. Whatever combinations of things were right for the most recent generation of films might not be right for future generations.

I am also reminded of the odd combinations of books that one can come across on tables in research libraries. Such mixes remind one of the fact that students and their professors may often need unpredictable combinations of reference materials to complete a given project that may be interesting in a context that might not have been anticipated as recently as months earlier.

The real genetic world is one that leans more toward moderate protectionism, restraint on monopolistic trends, and flexible social cooperative systems than toward the predatory capitalism or ruthless laissez faire competition advocated by Spencerian ideologies.

Platonic Monocultures, and Multiculturalism

The Platonic tradition has long esteemed static perfection or stable dynamic equilibria in nature and human affairs. Western terms of discourse have been built so much around this tradition that one speaks easily in terms of "ideal types," "optimal" outcomes, "purposes," and the like, and it implies that that which is valued should have a static quality. It is a tradition that has layered complex ontological theories over the child's at least partially natural tendency to classify, set goals, stereotype, assume absolute values. Instead of learning the true nature of these mental tools that can be helpful in childhood, during early growth, the child enters into a frozen symbiotic relationship with them and carries this relationship into adulthood.

It is obvious why central managers would want to simplify. They see it as their job to control, and centralized control is necessarily made difficult as the complexity increases of the system that is to be controlled. Indeed, where the diversity in life increase the world becomes even more difficult to visualize, understand, and discuss. Individuals who seeks to be authorities may feel smaller and smaller unless they can find someway to simplify the world in their thoughts and language or in their policies.

The small brain of the individual seeks to order all the flood of information that its five senses take in, while the continued dynamics of life in the long run depend on diversity. Life finds ways to organize itself.

It is obvious why leaders of political systems would want to simplify social life. It is an easy dream to imagine that the management of those below them would be easier if social life below them were orderly and predictable. It is also an easy dream to imagine that relationships between neighboring states and diplomacy would be easier if neighbors would think alike. This is one comforting view from above, looking down onto populations.

Empires have been built around seductive logic based on forms of Platonic idealisms. The Papal Monarchy of the Middle Ages did not survive its days of uncertain glory. National Socialism and Soviet communism did not survive. There are no historical or scientific reasons to believe that, even in purely practical terms, those who think of themselves as philosopher kings can build societies that are in the long run any more acceptable to humanity and more stable, or "better," than other cultural forms that are possible. Yale Professor James C. Scott has analyzed the reasons behind many planning disasters.

> Centrally managed social plans derail when they impose schematic visions that do violence to complex interdependencies that are not—and cannot be—fully understood. Further, the success of designs for social organization depends on the recognition that local, practical knowledge is as important as formal, epistemic knowledge.[5]

A human species made up of diverse cultures scattered over the earth's landscapes—each experimenting with solutions to the challenges of being human, discovering differences among themselves, swapping ideas and technologies between remote valleys and islands, across the barriers of language—may well have been the condition that pertained during the long march of human evolution. The evolutionary dynamics of the generation and recombination of novelties, selection, further recombination, and so on, that shaped the human species could well have been quite normal for organic life, even if many of the phenotypic traits that proved adaptive were cultural and arose from human imagination rather than from novelties in the DNA.

In this sense, an argument in favor of multiculturalism would be simply an argument for preserving the basic dynamic conditions that have fostered developments in human culture and consciousness.

Surely we have not yet learned all that we can from each other about the possibilities of being human. Surely there are still frontiers ahead where individualism can be better balanced with community, where the constructive creative potentials of individuals and groups can flower in brighter colors, where children can be better nourished and nurtured, where love within families and communities can be made more safe, where enlightenment can be better transmitted from generation to generation, where technology can be used wisely, where the tender foliage of truth and sincerity can be protected from trampling feet, where kindness will be reciprocated, where democracy can be of the people, by the people, and for the people.[6]

Notes

1. Of related interest, see Robert L. Heilbroner, *The Nature and Logic of Capitalism* (New York: Norton, 1985); Kenneth Lux, *Adam Smith's Mistake* (Boston: Shamabala, 1990); Karl Pribram, *A History of Economic Reasoning* (Baltimore: The Johns Hopkins University Press, 1983); Joseph A. Schumpeter, *History of Economic Analysis* (New York: Oxford University Press, 1954); Andrew Bard Schmooker, *The Illusion of Choice: How the Market Economy Shapes Our Destiny* (Albany: State University of New York Press, 1993).

2. See discussions and further references in Philip J. Regal, "Biotechnology jitters: will they blow over?" *Biotechnology Education* 1:2 (1989), pp. 51-55; Philip J. Regal, "Metaphysics in genetic engineering: cryptic philosophy and ideology in the 'science' of risk assessment," pp. 15-32 in Ad van Dommelen (ed), *Coping with Deliberate Release: The Limits of Risk Assessment* (Tilburg, The Netherlands: International Centre for Human and Public Affairs, (Social Studies of Science and Technology vol. 2, 1996).

3. One set of proponents of molecular guardianship are those scientists and their enthusiasts who are busy developing techniques to genetically engineer the human germ line (e.g. Lee M. Silver, *Remaking Eden* (New York: Avon Books, 1998). One could argue that the Gene-enriched or GenRich "post-humans" that they are working to create would add diversity to humanity. But in their vision, the new superior genetic types should socialize and interbreed to form new

ruling class. An inevitable part of biotechnological progress will be the reduction of most of humanity to an inferior status. There will be both social and reproductive isolation between the GenRich and the "naturals," who will have "as much romantic interest in each other as a current human would have for a chimpanzee." This is not then truly an ideology that intends to respect and foster cultural diversity on the planet. With flashy technology yoked to power and to spectacular utopian promises it is an ideology that could in effect direct all eggs of hope for a living humanism into a genetic basket.

4. Sarah Diamond, *Spiritual Warfare: The Politics of the Christian Right* (Boston: South End Press, 1989); Sarah Diamond, *Roads to Dominion* (New York: Guilford Press, 1995); James Davidson Hunter, *Culture Wars: The Struggle to Define America* (New York: Basic Books, 1991); Ellen Messer-Davidow, "Manufacturing the attack on liberalized higher education," *Social Text* 36 (1993), pp. 40-80; Jean Stefancic & Richard Delgado, *No Mercy: How Conservative Think Tanks and Foundations Changed America's Social Agenda* (Philadelphia: Temple University Press, 1996).

5. From the book cover—James C. Scott, *Seeing Like a State: How Certain Schemes to Improve the Human Condition have Failed* (New Haven: Yale University Press, 1998).

6. See also Philip J. Regal, *The Anatomy of Judgment* (Minneapolis: University of Minnesota Press, 1990).

7

MULTICULTURALISM—ECHOES OF DARWIN AND SPENCER

Andreas Rosenberg

We are again today, as countless times before, asking which is a right, good and efficient way for a multitude of humans to dwell together. We develop and propose models for that purpose, models such as representative democracy free enterprise, Christianity, addressing respectively the political, economic and religious aspects of the question. Both for efficient model building and in real life, we tend to divide the multitude into tribes or nations and identify and separate each by their specific culture. The concept of culture has been used for a long time and needs little explanation. It has often been used in the historical frame to describe the remarkable achievements of one or another nation states or league of states. For us Westerners, the Roman and Greek cultures have become definitions of the meaning for the term culture.

Recently, however, a new term has appeared, *multi–culturalism*, a term that has reached the status of buzzword, the highest level of significance in our culture. Estonian, a nation and culture I belong to, has a term for such concepts "uduangerjas," freely translated as eel-in-the fog. You are never sure whether you have caught the head or tail. Culture is generally defined in terms of language, literature and art although one has to be careful not to associate it too strongly with art forms such as folk dancing and costumes. That was the approach to culture in the former Soviet Union. You could suppress and obliterate any tribe or nation but as long as folk dancing was carried out in the local House of Culture, all was considered to be well with the tribal culture. Problems of definition mount with every new aspect you introduce into the culture concept. Can two cultures be separated when all members speak the same language? What are the necessary and sufficient conditions for defining a new culture?

We can more precisely and generally define culture as referring to a cultural phenotype (a concept describing the mental makeup characterizing individuals independent of the more well-known physical phenotype) based on language and religion but, most importantly, on memories represented by the new and very useful concept of memes, pieces of knowledge passed on from generation to generation through parents teaching their children. The similarity of memes to genes is clearly intended. Your inheritance of memes has, in analogy to the gene concept, dominant and recessive aspects and involves receiving memes from both of your parents. The only difference between genes and memes is that genes are practically immortal whereas memes have to be renewed and can be altered by circumstances.

If we use the cultural phenotype concept to define our understanding of the scope of the culture concept, where does multiculturalism fall? I think of a picture of thirty to forty cultures, well separated and each existing within the boundaries of a nation state.

The Europe of today, for example, is not an example of the multiculturalism we are debating in this country. Our concept of multiculturalism refers to several of cultural phenotypes coexisting in relatively random distribution within the boundaries of our present state, the United States. The most interesting point about this concept of multiculturalism is the fact that it carries with it an enormous *a priori* value judgment embedded in the definition. It is considered either a wonderful or a dangerous deviation from the assimilation mode that the majority in this country perceives as unavoidable and laudable.

Of course, we must realize that there is no such thing as a totally homogeneous culture. Culture is the expression of an ongoing dynamic process The cultures of the world have all evolved from the same root. The phenomenon of the creation of new cultures or fusion of previously separate entities into one is a process uncannily similar to formation of species so eloquently described by Darwin. Within an existing culture, physical isolation, dialect formation, and religious regroupings continually create local subcultures by a process quite similar to the way in which physical restrictions lead to development of variations within a species. The situation, of course, is more complex for the culture space than for the biological space. We have to deal with non-physical, conceptual structures such as nation states or unions of states. Does a nation state with official language immediately define a dominating culture? Is language the deciding factor? Do Germany and Austria clearly two states but with a common language represent two cultures? We cannot allow our inquiry to become too broad and span all over the globe.

Let us narrow our considerations to a case where some specific questions can be asked. The specifications and assumptions we propose to use have to be quite narrowly defined; however we recognize in advance their arbitrary nature which allows us to return later to reconsider our calculations and modify our premises.

We assume we have a sovereign state, the United States, with a population of immigrants and descendants of immigrants (with the exception of Native Americans) We have a common currency and an official language, English. We have a secular constitution freedom of religion and laws applicable evenly to all inhabitants. In this commonly-called melting pot, the cultural memes of immigrants persist and thus cultural heritage is with regularity resurrected, religion and separate customs re-affirmed. Children are educated by parents and memes are transferred. This is the process of subculture formation, the variation of species in Darwinian sense. Such subcultures have two alternative scenarios for further development. The first assumes such subcultures are temporary phenomena—fluctuations of the melting pot. The other scenario assumes that at one point the differences between the subculture and the parent culture have become such that the members of the subculture consider themselves to be a permanent separate culture instead a subdivision of the main culture. This is the picture envisioned by most advocates of multiculturalism. In extreme it is represented by the Quebec phenomena.

The choice between these two scenarios outlined above form the focus and goal our discussion in this paper. The question we are asking is not if either of the two processes is more desirable than the other one. This would lead to value judgments. We can analyze only measurable outcomes for different models based on our two scenarios. We can ask and estimate which of the models is more efficient in terms of production of goods, communication and information transfer, more access to personal choice of careers and lifestyle. Which model is more viable in terms of absence of conflict, which model leads to higher cultural output. How can we go about to compare the models in terms more quantitative than the anecdotal stories. The formalism of testing and comparing such models has been worked out for studies of species competition and survival in the sense of the Darwinian selection This method is based on the *game theory* and the great name in the field is John Maynard Smith, who introduced new concepts such as "survival value" and "evolutionarily stable configurations of multiple species within the same boundaries." The second of these two concepts is a transformation of our multicultural model into the physical-survival space.

This approach using the *game theory* to evaluate our models corresponding to the two scenarios outlined above is apt to be criticized as a forbidden transformation of a simple biological model to the plane of social sciences. Such a transformation may lead to something like social Darwinism, a thoroughly discredited approach the study of human communities. We have here to stress that one does not have to borrow the biological model of survival and the concepts of food procurement and competition for territory from Smith and Darwin as Spencer did. We will borrow only the formalism of the model, but move it from survival, proliferation, and breeding to the culture/society space.

We will also limit our discussion to principles, logic, and the possible outcomes, avoiding mathematical details, which, although trivial, tend to overwhelm many readers. Let us examine the workings of the method in a very simple but highly relevant example for future discussion of minority populations.

Consider a homogeneous majority culture with 95 percent of inhabitants and a minority cultural phenotype making up the missing 5 percent, a minority with its own religion and memes passed on from generation to generation. The minority phenotype is presumed to be distributed randomly within the majority population. Let us first study the survival of memes and thus the culture. We assume that 50 percent of both populations are female and the contacts between male and female are random. The random contacts represent the heart of the Maynard Smith method where the population moves continuously in a random manner leading to random encounters between individuals. We give a probability, for example 1:20, for a contact between male and female leading to marriage and children. Marriage results in passing on of memes. Mixed marriages lead to passing on 50 percent of the memes while homogeneous marriages lead to passing on 100 percent of memes. We see immediately without any calculations that in a random mating pattern the probability of homogeneous marriages is very small and we can easily calculate that the memes are diluted and lost in a certain number of generations, the number depending on what percentage of memes has to be preserved to assure the survival of the cultural identity. If the lowest necessary amount that needs to be retained is set to 25 percent of memes, we see that after three generations, we are below the critical level. The Maynard Smith model formalizes encounter numbers and the probability for outcomes, and we can calculate in terms of probability how long memes will survive in different types of population mixes and time frames. This can become mathematically quite complex for models with higher fractions of minorities and varying probabilities.

The problem of the danger to minority memes resulting from uncontrolled breeding has been perceived by minorities and the major variables influencing the outcome in the random encounter model have been identified. The minorities have made practical efforts to change the workings of the model. We can increase the probability of homogeneous marriages between minority culture phenotypes by physically moving from random population mix to local segregation of the minority. Another variable that can be changed is the probability of mating and marriage in case of heterogeneous encounters. We see that minorities such as Hasidic Jews and Amish settlers have used both variables by voluntary ghetto formation and religious taboos against marriages outside their culture.

The example shows the basic functioning of the calculation method based on the game theory. The conclusions drawn from this simple example are however quite important. They state that the preservation of permanent populations of cultural phenotypes that are very different from the majority population is always precarious, and that in order to survive and preserve the meme structures the minorities have to worry about the mating and concentration of their populations.

This in no way answers the question about the two scenarios we are interested in. An answer to this question will tell us how countries with multiple independent cultures will fare compared to countries where the same resources are present in a culturally homogeneous population.

The analysis of such scenarios is a vastly more complex problem. For that purpose, we preserve as the first step the model of a total population consisting of a majority and a minority component and the pattern of random encounters. However, instead of courting and mating with marriage we will have to consider a number of additional productive exchanges associated with these random encounters. Let us first some of the most important ones:

(1) conflict or avoidance of conflict

(2) information exchange

(3) cultural exchange

(4) multi-individual work projects

(5) partnership formation

There are, of course, many more possible outcomes of an encounter. The next step is to define and evaluate the encounter results in terms of the progress or effect they produce. Mating produced children and transferred memes, so we could give the value 1 for homogeneous marriage and 0.5 for heterogeneous marriage. (We have for the moment not considered the effects of differential fertility). The assignment of values to all types of outcomes resulting from an encounter is difficult and often becomes arbitrary in which case we have to reevaluate our choices and try many schemes of values. Let us consider *exchange of information*, an encounter listed as the second variable above. There are two possibilities. First that individuals belonging either to minority or majority speak different languages and the second possibility is that they speak one common language, allowing them to communicate. The first case of different languages leads to positive outcome for a homogeneous encounter and negative for a heterogeneous encounter. We can easily see that a population of 50 percent of one phenotype and 50 percent of the second phenotype defined as able to speak only their own language leads to practical cessation of information transfer and collapse of a modem society. I think all of us have realized this on our first visit to Japan trying to figure out which toilet is for men and which for women. We have to adopt either a Swiss model of multiple obligatory languages or drift toward physical separation as seems to be taking place in Belgium. The next variable, *avoidance of conflict*, presents a far more complex situation than the previous variable, *ability to communicate*. The presence of conflict upon encounter clearly yields a negative value, and the absence of conflict can be given a positive value but how are we to estimate the probability of conflict in a random encounter? The probability for conflict varies depending on the value of other variables associated with the phenotypes meeting and on the results of exchanges of other types taking place during the same encounter. Logically, I am sure evidence can be found to verify that the highest probability for conflict resulting from a meeting between individuals appears when the individuals cannot communicate due to language problems, when they belong to different religious communities, when they follow different ethical systems and, finally, when they have physical characteristics that easily distinguish them. We see that the *conflict probability* is a complex variable.

When we consider the variable we call *partnership formation,* it stands out clearly that the probability of positive outcome is influenced by both the language variable and the absence of conflict. We can ask what forms the basis of trust necessary for partnership formation? Probably the degree of common memes present in the individuals. A partner has to have an inkling how the mind of the other, prospective, partner works. We see clearly, even without the necessity of assigning to all these encounter results numbers and calculating corresponding probabilities, that the heterogeneous encounters seem to be doomed to be less positive by all criteria we have considered up to this point.

In terms of evaluation of the possible contribution to the effective functioning of the society the heterogeneous encounters seem to be less successful. Before leaving these variables we have to realize that even the apparently simplest variable, *mating probability,* does not have but one consequence, that of diminishing meme transfer. The negative effect of the loss of a strong presence of memes may on the other hand lead to diminished possibilities for conflict an extra consequence of encounters, the contribution of which has to be accounted in a more detailed model. Still, all the characteristics we have evaluated up to now—*consequence of mating, communications, conflict and partnership formation*—favor the homogeneous encounter and point to formation of an homogeneous society as the preferred alternative, We have to consider other variables to find the positive contributions produced by the heterogeneous encounters.

We will have to turn to the purely cultural variables not related to the efficiency with which a society works and produces goods.

The evaluation of cultural exchange of encounters presents other type of problems. We will have to consider a new type of communication barrier not related to language necessarily. If an individual has inherited interest in and love for country Western music, he may not relate well to an ardent lover of Bach. He may not buy tickets for a performance of Bach and the Bach lover may not choose to listen to country music. This difference in choice of cultural experiences, however, is not all negative. Encounter of heterogeneous kind between different cultural phenotypes presents a learning possibility. If the whole population would be homogenous in terms of loving Western music, where would a nascent Bach lover ever find information and fellowship. Thus the possibility of learning by transfer of cultural experiences gives heterogeneous encounters high positive value. The interactions between different forms and modes of cultural expression present further intriguing problems. What is more advantageous, having poetry in twenty languages or a twenty times larger variation of poetry in one language? We have to analyze the ability of any mixture of different cultures to support the necessary cultural organization to provide for the expression of alternatives in culture. This evaluation will contain another critical variable—that of the preservation of culture. For example if the memes of Native Americans should dissipate by assimilation, the loss would mean an absolute loss of the experiences associated with these memes which would be a thoroughly negative contribution. Similar, in fact, to extinction of species. On the other hand the Spanish culture, the heart of which lies outside United States, would have an independent existence and continued production of memes regardless of the fate of the Spanish cultural minority in the United States.

In summary, we conclude from this very superficial evaluation of possible variables determining the consequences of encounters in the basic random encounter model that even without detailed assessment of probabilities we already can say that the factors associated with economy, production, information transfer, and conflict avoidance heavily favor homogeneous encounters. This fact together with mating patterns consequently points toward a homogeneous culture in equilibrium with temporary subcultures as the logically better outcome for our two-scenario model. In order to shift our calculations and estimates towards different outcome we would have to compensate the economy and technology-related encounter variables with very strong positive cultural contributions favoring heterogeneous encounters. These putative positive contributions all have to come from the process of cultural enrichment and the expansion of individual life style options. The question is whether their values can balance the heavily negative load of factors associated with efficiency and economy? The other day I came across a Rotary handout that in full color praised Singapore, the host city for the next Rotary International Conference, as the beautiful multicultural city. The major points of success were described as presence of law and order, the existence an official language, and freedom of religion. The multiculturalism we think about was reduced to the wonderful picture presented by the multicultural restaurants existing side by side. This cannot be the reason and justification for existence of multicultural states. It became clear in reading further that the cultural offerings accessible to every one where those translated into the official language or presented by visual or culinary means.

Before moving to discussion of the conclusions of our qualitative assessment of the viability of different scenarios for the future of the multicultural model, we have to evaluate the personal satisfaction of members of a culture when operating only within such culture and avoiding the necessity of acquiring new types of memes. How much positive value can we assign to a minority-minority encounter the pleasure of recognizing fellow members of a separate community. If we assign this variable high value, we can of course balance any of the negative contributions from heterogeneous encounters. However in order to maximize such a contribution we also have to maximize the number of encounters between minority phenotype. This must lead to a segregation of the minority population, a Chinatown syndrome. In our premises for the U.S. model we excluded that possibility. If the personal satisfaction contribution cannot be satisfied by formation of secluded communities, the negative encounter factors seem to overwhelm our model.

The only way to balance this negativity is to move and change the restrictions of our model so as to diminish the major negative factors associated with heterogeneous encounters. We have to change the premises in such a way that the negative variables can be balanced by the positive cultural exchange factors.

The absence of communication is one of the major negative factors, so we start by

(1) introduction of an official and common language (English in this case) providing all cultures the opportunity to learn their language as the second language. The Singapore and Indian model.

To avoid conflict situations, another highly negative variable, we have to add to easy communications a system of functional ethical rules, common to all, by

(2) affirmation of the absolute dominance of a secular set of laws over various culture-based sets of rules and taboos.

This may provide the best basis for partnership formation between individuals from different cultural backgrounds. To further strengthen the mutually acceptable set of behavioral rules; we have to

(3) maintain a very clear separation between religion and the organization of the state.

By these changes in the total framework for our multicultural model, the major variables contributing negatively to the encounter statistics will be greatly reduced and the cultural enrichment factors can balance the other divisive features of a multicultural society.

What we have learned from our qualitative scientific encounter model is that multiculturalism has to be defined carefully and be restricted in application otherwise it will lead either to conflict of Yugoslavian type or the Quebec type of separation. With restrictions, along the lines outlined above, the multicultural society holds great promise. It certainly is not an accident that the restrictions so essential for the success of a multicultural state are all basic tenets of humanism. The Darwinian model in Maynard Smith formulation is useful in evaluating the functioning of cultures and can lead to a model representing an acceptable equilibrium between different cultural impulses. This equilibrium can be very creative for future development through the inherent tensions it has and the competition it produces.

References:

Charles Darwin, *The Origin of Species* (London, 1859).

John Maynard Smith, *Evolution and the Theory of Games* (New York: Cambridge University Press, 1982).

8

DEMOCRACY, UNIVERSALISM, AND MULTICULTURALISM AT CENTURY'S END

Khoren Arisian

Universalism Vindicated: The Pinochet Effect

Exactly a year ago, British authorities detained onetime Chilean dictator, General Augusto Pinochet, in London where he had gone for rest, relaxation, and medical treatment. On October 16, 1998, Pinochet was suddenly arrested on a Spanish court warrant alleging the deaths and disappearances of more than three thousand dissidents during his seventeen-year rule which began in a bloody military coup against Chile's democratically elected socialist President, Salvador Allende, in 1973. Allende died during the attack on the Presidential palace, whether by suicide or murder is still moot.

The House of Lords ruled that Pinochet was not entitled to immunity from arrest under a British law protecting former heads of state. The British High Court determined, according to one newspaper account, that the retired General "is liable to prosecution for acts of torture committed after Britain ratified the Torture Convention in 1988," despite the fact he was a foreign head of state at the time. Chile has tried unrelentingly to challenge the extradition proceedings. Pinochet's attorney, for example, refutes allegations that the former Chilean dictator tortured a victim with electric shock, even arguing casuistically that "Instantaneous death does not amount to torture," the victim in question having died instantly! What is at issue, according to the Spanish judge who made the original extradition demand against Pinochet, are "principles of independent justice." If he is convicted and sentenced, thereby establishing a precedent in international law, Pinochet's fate will be decisive: nations that abide by the rule of law will no longer be able to serve as safe havens for former murderous dictators. Since his departure, the fear in Chile of military retaliation in response to his imprisonment abroad has psychologically abated; citizens and politicians are again breathing more freely and courageously.

"Principles of independent justice" is a phrase that resonates with universalist overtones: a tyrannical ruler cannot cavalierly murder his own citizens anymore and expect no judicatory consequence when he leaves the borders of his own country. All exiled dictators are hereafter at risk. Among those who realize this is Slobodan Milosevic, who has chosen to remain in his own country rather than risk traveling beyond it.

The Tragedy of Kosovo

That relations between political states must be founded upon the regular observance of human rights rather than mere sovereignty, is a universalist outlook born of respect for the individual. This imperative was savagely thrust aside in the tragic fate visited upon

Kosovo at the beginning of the second week in April, 1999. President Milosevic of Yugoslavia, having orchestrated the traumatic travails of Serbia's ethnic Albanians in the formerly autonomous province of Kosovo—despite NATO's launch of the largest air war in Europe since 1945 (complemented by the largest mass deportations of a victimized population)—suddenly declared a unilateral cease-fire in prospective deference to the Orthodox Easter later in the week, in effect inviting NATO to take supposedly similar peaceful measures. What chutzpah! The nineteen constituent countries of the recently enlarged North Atlantic Treaty Organization, originally created for the purpose of executing defensive responses to aggressors against any of its members, found itself instead on one side of a civil war—an awkwardly uncharacteristic and officially inappropriate position to assume on the eve of its fiftieth anniversary even if a humanitarian crisis of stupendous proportions morally justified such a stance.

The Balkan predicament since the sudden implosion of Communism in 1989 can be seen as a veritable case study in multiculturalism gone awry—how ethnic diversity can degenerate into separatism, then into conflict and finally into ethnic cleansing. When Communism collapsed in Yugoslavia, the resulting vacuum was filled by resurgent nationalisms that fed on unresolved cultural differences going back centuries among Catholic Croats, Orthodox Serbs, and Muslim Albanians and others. An atavistic retribalization took hold even as other parts of the world were celebrating the onset of economic globalization. (The Orwellian dictum, that some people are officially to be categorized and treated as less than equal to others, was, let us recall, the operating premise of the American government in the nineteenth century when its cavalry was ordered time after time to subdue and decimate the native Indian tribes of the continent.)

The twentieth century, which really started in 1914 with WW I and ended with Communism's disintegration seventy-five   years later, has been marked by continuous warfare and punctuated by a variety of horrendous atrocities. The first real holocaust occurred in 1915 when one million Armenians were systematically slaughtered by the Ottoman Turks; the last great atrocity of this century, what Elie Wiesel has termed a near-holocaust, took place in Kosovo, as we have noted, in the month of April of the last year of the current millennium. Sandwiched between these two tragic events were the Nazi Holocaust in which six million Jews and other "undesirables" like gays and gypsies perished, followed decades later by equally horrific, if less extensive, equivalents in Cambodia, Rwanda, and elsewhere. Surely the moral scale of human life has diminished in the wake of these barbaric outbreaks despite a growing awareness of the universality of human rights throughout the last half of the twentieth century.

Culture and Politics

Culture's content is extremely complex and varied, signifying the totality of human behavior, thought and practice: personal taste and refinement; the intellectual, artistic and literary aspects of human activity; institutionalized norms and traits learned and transmitted from generation to generation; styles of human relationship characterizing the socialization process; the psychological dynamics of personality and character development; preferred moral patterns and value systems; and so on.

Cultural pluralism refers to that condition in which definable minority groups participate in the dominant society while maintaining their cultural differences which typically include ethnicity, language and religion. All these factors contribute to but do not exhaust human identity. What Milosevic aimed to achieve in Kosovo was cultural destruction, the attempted obliteration of the very identity of a whole people; cultural pluralism, in effect, was canceled. That birds of a feather like to gather together and keep others out still has truth to it.

Generally speaking, cultural studies have not traditionally included political history, these two academic disciplines being treated as separate fields of knowledge. Nonetheless politics and culture are mutually implicated in one another in real life. When a number of Albanians fled across the Macedonian border to be taken in by a substantial minority of their ethnic brethren, the Orthodox Serb majority became rattled and annoyed. Hostile outbreaks of a minor sort between these two groups ensued almost immediately. Thus did political turmoil mortally imperil the viability of cultural pluralism in the Balkans at century's end.

Time was, of course, when Yugoslavia's cultural diversity was artificially propped up by Tito's Communist regime—in retrospect an artificial arrangement that could not last, allowing centuries-old unsettled scores to re-emerge and be infused into a resurgent nationalism. Samuel Huntington's celebrated thesis in *The Clash of Civilizations and the Remaking of World Order* is that as globalization exfoliates, the importance of political borders supposedly fades, causing people to identify instead with cultural factors closer to home—like ethnic groups and/or familiar religious affiliations. At such historic junctures, nationalistic fervency can be transferred to traditional behaviors that now occupy center stage. In such a detribalized situation, a transcultural sensibility, normally the rational prelude to an ethos of moral universalism, is atavistically delayed.

Cultural Diversity and the First World's Parliament of Religions

Contemplating such matters as the above can profitably turn one's attention to the first World's Parliament of Religions in 1893 the centenary observance of which, like the Parliament itself, was held in Chicago. Taking inspiration from this singular event exactly 100 years earlier, the centennial organizers projected a laudable goal and vision: creation of a global ethic in the form of a Declaration extolling the universality of human rights and responsibilities which, it was hoped, might be publicly invoked as a force for peace and unity among peoples in a less conflicted, more humane twenty-first century. The 1993 Declaration acknowledged and celebrated the diversity of cultures and religions throughout the world while insisting that such diversity need not preclude mutual agreement or certain norms of civil conduct that have universal applicability. A few years ago, international financier George Soros contended that the concept of an open society "which not only recognizes the multiplicity of cultures and traditions but actively advocates pluralism, could serve as a unifying principle for our global society." Soros noted, however, that this salvific concept thus far was "neither recognized nor accepted"—therein lies the rub and, by implication, the humanist challenge. How then, might we go about advocating on behalf of an open, pluralistic society that can, in different guises and in different cultural contexts, serve as a robust microcosm of what a global village might look like?

What Sparked the Centenary Celebration?

What actuated the 1993 World's Parliament organizers was a mixture of alarm and urgency. The Gulf War, after all, was fresh in everyone's memory. If organized religion was ever to become a unified force to be taken seriously in the future, it had to emerge from its frequently cocooned enclaves, however large or small, and effectively connect the energies of humanity's inner life with its outward activities in search of a materially more equitable and morally sensitized world.

Hans Küng, the extraordinarily vigorous Swiss Catholic theologian, very much his own man and one who does not shun controversy (for which regularly exhibited tendency the Vatican withdrew his credentials as a Church theologian), was delegated to create the first draft of the Declaration, subsequently critically and extensively modified by colleagues and organizers of the centenary observance of the 1893 Parliament. The Preamble to the initial Declaration was published in Jone Johnson's essay in the 1998 issue of *Humanism Today* in which the present predicament of the world is suitably deplored, a consensus for a global ethic affirmed as a common dimension among the religions of the world, and moral equality attributed axiomatically to the earth's entire community of living beings. The Declaration's preamble is blessedly free of theology or theism, being in its totality a universal ethical proclamation resting ultimately upon the intangible reality of humanity's innate moral sense.

Apparently, during the wide-ranging discussions preceding the final form of the Declaration, Küng stated unequivocally that the great majority of armed conflicts in the world are either largely or partly fueled by ancient unresolved arguments over religious and related differences. Religion, said Küng, frequently provides the inspiration, overtones, background, vocabulary and support for revived and intensified hatred and strife. Küng concluded oracularly: "There will be no peace in the world until there is peace among the religions." A long wait is likely. One can easily be reminded here of Lord Acton's dictum: "There is nothing so fearsome as one lone

Calvinist in possession of the Truth." Küng's blunt admission that deep religious convictions can sometimes have a murderous downside that encourages violence towards those not of the same faith (e.g., the late Ayatollah's fatwah on the life of author Salman Rushdie) should give everyone pause, especially in view of the naïve American inclination to believe that traditional organized religion is somehow an inherent, if not unalloyed good, an always reliable vehicle for moral order.

In the planning leading up to the centenary celebration, Rabbi Herman Schaalman, one of the major participants in organizing this gargantuan event, put forth the official summons, saying:

> What struggles to arise out of the past might become our shared future of mutual hearing and understanding, of mutual openness, of unprecedented willingness to acknowledge and accept others in all their differentness?

Milosevic's answer to such a question would not be hard to imagine.

If the proximate objective of ecumenism is to overcome differences for the sake of organizational unity, the much more open-ended purpose of the 1893 and 1993 Parliaments was interreligious dialogue aimed at stimulating mutual enlightenment rather than the overcoming of differences. Beyond the cordiality of both Parliaments, differences in the real world have nonetheless remained flashpoints for conflict. Indeed, during the seventeen days in September, 1893 during which the first Parliament met as part of the great Chicago Exposition, a Unitarian minister in attendance, Joseph Henry Allen, noted that at the very moment the Parliament meetings were underway, battles were raging between Muslims and Hindus in Bombay and Calcutta, Spanish Christians and Moors were on the verge of war in North Africa, Armenians were being persecuted by Turks and Russians alike, Jews were being subjected to pogroms in eastern Europe, and Presbyterians and Papists were fighting each other in Ireland!

While during the multiple gatherings of the centenary observance in Chicago, at least two thirds of the conflicts then in progress throughout the world, most notably in Bosnia and Kashmir, exhibited a strong religious element which the delegates publicly and ruefully acknowledged.

Küng's Global Ethic enshrines universals: beneath culturally specific differences which there's no valid reason to jettison, we still touch ground together at the bedrock of human interdependence. The leading public religious celebrity at the centenary convocation whose words echoed Küng's was Tibet's exiled Dalai Lama whose inclusive style and personality were revealed in his extemporaneous remarks transcribed as follows:

> In spite of our differences, we are the same human being. We all have a right to happiness. Most powerful source and resource for happiness is within ourselves....We need to implement our inner resource with compassion [which is possible to do] without religion. Secular ethics are okay....[Tibetan, like much of Buddhism, being essentially atheistic].

Spiritually central for the Dalai Lama is the ethical factor in everyday experience. Needless to elaborate, references were made in this regard to the humanistic spirit of Martin Luther King, Jr., 1993 marking, coincidentally, the twenty-fifth anniversary of his assassination. In his memorable "I have a dream" speech of 1963, he had made clear that what's chiefly of value in human beings is the content of their character, not their color or any other secondary identification. Nothing reveals our enduring uniqueness more strikingly than our moral outlook and consequent behavior in relation to one another. There were, as well, remembrances of the first UN Secretary General, Dag Hammarskjold, a politically astute peacemaker who was at heart—like Julian Huxley—a secular mystic.

Küng was a constant presence at the 1993 centennial, reminding delegates of their *public* responsibility as religious intellectuals. As such it's not our duty to do the work of government or of politics, he said, except to participate robustly at the citizen level: but in light of the moral universalism that binds us at our shared depth of being, we need to keep calling attention to what needs to be done in the world. For example, said Küng, a number of recognized world religious leaders warmly supported the agenda of the 1992 Rio Conference on the Environment whose leading mantra was that because the earth bears us all, we in turn should care for it actively and together. Meager though our separate resources may be, he went on, we still have the power of speech and of the written word: we can advocate, we can demonstrate, we can help shape public opinion. Is not such counsel, finally, a classic prophetic imperative? Prophecy finds its natural footing in the public sphere.

"The Feast of Reason"

If the original World's Parliament of Religions signaled for the modern era the beginning of international interreligious cooperation and dialogue along startlingly liberal lines, its 1993 reincarnation confirmed and extended that enterprise. It's instructive to note that at the 1990 Congress of the International Association for Religious Freedom (the IARF itself being a spin-off from the 1893 World's Parliament of Religions), Küng—a few years before he would also be a key figure at the 1993 Parliament, asked the assembled delegates: "Should it not be possible for all religions to agree [that]...the good for human persons is what helps them to be truly human?" Such obviously humanist sentiments had been prefigured by Jenkin Lloyd George at the 1893 World's Parliament where Jones, then a Chicago Unitarian minister, served as the Parliament's secretary, crafting the first draft of its program and enhancing it with participation by Jews and Asians: "not the supernatural Christ, but the natural soul of man was the center round which the Parliament moved," he asserted. (It should be explained here that the Colombian Exposition of 1893, popularly known as the Chicago World's Fair, was bolstered by a series of twenty international congresses in several fields of human learning of which religion was one—the World's Parliament.) Renowned Ethical Culture Leader and Unitarian minister, Anna Garlin Spencer, who attended the congress, referred ecstatically to "the new scientific element in religion," an element largely notable today by its absence. Julia Ward Howe, also in attendance, vigorously insisted that "nothing is religious which puts one individual absolutely above others, and...one sex above another," thus registering her rejection of inequality in human relationships, a cardinal democratic tenet of the humanist way of life. No wonder that in a book on the subject published in 1986, historian Richard Seager describes the 1893 Parliament as "a rite of passage for America, a transition from an era when the United States was often considered, however inaccurately, to be a Christian, hence Protestant, nation into an era marked by increasing religious pluralism." That pluralism, of course, continues to grow and flourish as a new millennium approaches.

Jones, Frank Lloyd Wright's uncle, was a prickly prophet who proclaimed that an altogether new religion was called for, one that would bear no traditional denominational designation but enlist the universal ethical and spiritual sympathies of the unchurched along with Reform Jews, Ethical Culturists and assorted religious liberals ready to relinquish even those mildly sectarian affiliations in favor of, possibly, a "great prophetic Free Church of America." He saw the Parliament as a challenge in particular to Unitarians whom he perceived as walking hesitatingly at best along the "ragged edge of Christendom." Unitarianism, he argued, needed to expire so that this new broader mood might emerge from "the splendid inspiration of natural religion, of *universal* faith" (echoes of eighteenth century deism). Whereas other denominations were theologically inclined, said Jones, this new religious movement would instead be "allied to questions of anthropology." Elizabeth Cady Stanton, also present at the Parliament, made the same point in equally expansive terms:

> The new religion will teach the dignity of human nature and its infinite possibilities for development. It will teach the solidarity of the race—that all must rise and fall as one. Its creed will be justice, liberty, equality for all the children of the earth.

All this was exuberant creative visioning, much too radical and ahead of its time to make institutional headway within any existing liberal religious group. What should have happened—in my view, a huge historical loss—would have been the separate establishment of an Association of Free Religious Societies of North America.

To its everlasting credit the first World's Parliament of Religions did not tend toward advocating syncretism, the artificial effort to combine and reconcile, inevitably at a cost to integrity, diverse tenets and practices of world religions into some innocuous middle-of-the-road stew. As the aforementioned Rev. Allen put it similarly in regard to the same point: it was fortunate that the Parliament's overriding purpose was not to attempt to merge all the great religions into a "flavorless, neutral compound" and instead regularly encouraged its delegates to hear each other out. Thereby could one maintain one's own set of philosophic or theological principles while seeing some of them in a new light precisely because of the openness of the dialogic encounter, exactly what a *principled* pluralism comprises.

The 1893 conclave was thus unique in several respects, not least of all in that it was the first undertaking of its kind to include representatives from most of the world's religions, especially those in Asia. The cumulative upshot: the Parliament proved to be a big plus for the study of comparative religion, while it also proved to be at once the most remarkable of the several congresses at the Exposition and the most popular with the press and public alike, attracting audiences of upwards of 4,000 at each of its daily sessions. It's worth adding that Jones arranged separate congresses for the Free Religious Association, Ethical Culture, and the hottest scientific and intellectual hypothesis in the wake of Darwinism's advent—Evolution! So it was that the Parliament succeeded in highlighting both religious differences and religious common ground. One of the several speakers, Professor Chakravati, expressed his personal delight that at the heart of the World's Fair amidst its exaltation of modern civilization's vast material progress, provision had been abundantly made for the "feast of reason and the flow of soul".

Summing Up

If the first Parliament of the World's Religions represented the dawn of modern religious pluralism, then, as mentioned earlier, we are today far more advanced down that road. America's ethnic diversity has accelerated amazingly; no longer are we a largely Anglo-Saxon, mainstream-Protestant nation. We Americans have historically assumed that we are a continuous melting pot, our preference being assimilation, not multiculturalism. As for tension between assimilation and pluralism, it's ongoing. If there are now more Muslims in the United States than Episcopalians; if in the social hall of an Islamic mosque in Quincy, Massachusetts not far from the birthplace of flinty John Quincy Adams, the Stars and Stripes, Islamic, and Massachusetts state flags are all flown together on special occasions, do we consequently face a national identity crisis, a disuniting of the country, as historian Arthur Schlesinger, Jr. feared not long ago? Hardly! *E pluribus unum* is the motto of the world's first and only universal nation based on the abstract notion of individual human rights—the United States of America. Probably more than any other single nation in history, America is, in Edward L. Ericson's words, "creatively linked by origin and nature to all other nations and cultures." Contrary to what some might see as fragmentation in American life, the truth may be that on balance we are, as Alan Wolfe felicitously phrases it in the title of his recent book, *One Nation After All*. The United States is the most unified of countries precisely because it is the most individually diverse.

Multiculturalism: A Critique

Today's multicultural imperative is too often, and sometimes irresponsibly invoked, to imply that culture is very nearly fixed and impervious rather than dynamic and porous. For the most part, culture in the modern era has a plasticity that primitive culture does not: modern-day human communities, in other words, are simply no longer as discrete and complete in themselves as some still choose to imagine. So when multiculturalism in a globalizing world assumes iconic proportions in an age, like ours, of political correctness and morphs into an orthodoxy of sorts, it becomes dangerously misguided. Multiculturalism becomes inane when, say, it decrees that students in a public school be divided into groups largely on the basis of race or ethnicity rather than freely mingling with one another as individuals. A multicultural outlook that sanctifies social parallelism rather than interaction is no longer diverse but subversive of democracy's foundational intent—namely, that we are first and foremost a nation of individuals, not of separate cultures. America was not founded as a Republic in 1789 on the ancient premise of tribal kinship but on the modern universalist premise of human equality and personal freedom, however imperfectly this ideal has so far been realized. A mature democratic society, therefore, is one that is greater than the sum of the individuals comprising it. Recall again how King's vision of an interracial egalitarianism elevated the cause of civil rights to the plane of an ethical universalism. Morally disruptive actions were consequently directed against American apartheid in order to engender more freedom and thus diversity for the largely disenfranchised segments of the citizenry.

How Does This Novel Universalist Attitude Work Itself Out in Practice?

In 1858, Abraham Lincoln noted that the number of recent immigrants (at the time, mostly of European origin) was roughly equal to the number of descendants of the founding generation of the Republic. In appropriating the legacy of inalienable individual rights, a common spiritual bond among succeeding generations would thereby be continuously precipitated. This abstract idea is, of course, movingly demonstrated every time a group of immigrants from diverse backgrounds publicly take the oath of full citizenship. Not blood, but conviction in the worth and dignity of every individual as a free universal being, whatever one's origin—not as an unwitting representative of a particular culture—is what constitutes the ever changing palette of American life. Amazingly enough, as we rapidly approach the end of the twentieth century, nearly one U.S. resident in ten is foreign-born, similar to the proportion recorded 150 years ago when the Census Bureau first asked people their place of birth, a fact to which Lincoln would allude eight years later. In American life, individualism ultimately trumps culturalism.

E pluribus unum signifies that in a mature democracy, individuals choose to transcend their personal and cultural differences in a common citizenship. Put otherwise, multiculturalism is neither a necessary antidote to racism nor necessarily helpful in establishing a national democratic identity. And as for the so-called "culture wars" of the 1990s, they were deliberately contrived so as to sow divisiveness and thereby enable a predominantly rightist identity politics to replace an impersonal economics as American society's secular focus and driving force.

Postscript

During the remarkable period, then, between 1776 and 1789, a universal ethic that implied such an end as mentioned above was painfully struggling to surface in the minds of the colonists: the notion that everyone of any descent is somehow equally worthy of freedom. Women, Native Americans, black slaves, to be sure, were not factored into that equation, but the logic of the universalist principle so enunciated has made it clear over succeeding generations that differences among individuals demand freedom, and that freedom in turn generates ever more diversity and, therefore, an ethical call for mutually attributed equality. Meanwhile, if the rulers and the ruled are to be kept in civilized balance—a major point of debate in the *Federalist Papers*—there have to be limits to what they can do to one another. Government is a necessary guarantor of those limits but, as James Madison strongly insisted, must itself observe the constitutional limits of its statutory powers.

The English heritage of opposition to arbitrary rule and of ultimate faith in self-governance on the part of the citizenry proved decisive in the formation of the new democratic view of human nature: a distinctly secular conception at the heart of which lies a nonsectarian spiritual ideal—the freedom and development of the individual in community with others—one's right to "the pursuit of happiness". The American idea thus ends on a note of universal spiritual idealism ("spiritual" here refers at once to the residual uniqueness of the individual and his/her interdependence; since individuality implies sociality, each of us emerges differently from our interaction with others). The United States considered as a whole is less a congeries of cultures and more a gathering of individuals who live in multiple "life-worlds," to quote Howard Radest. Unfortunate or not, it's neither in our history nor in our collective character to have arranged an equivalent of Canada's laudable experiment with Aboriginal peoples; multiculturalism is simply not the American style, assimilation is.

Yet, as previously intimated, multiculturalism has become a politically correct dogma. What this means is social parallelism, merely the latest incarnation of the group psychology syndrome that began arraying itself against personal individuality during the coercive McCarthyist period of the 1950s when moral courage was in short supply. Multiculturalism fails adequately to encourage critical, inquiring openness between groups. It often stops or deflects real conversation between the members thereof: certain topics cannot be discussed in certain quarters, or if they can be, there is only a certain manner in which the conversation is allowed to proceed. This is no way for people to learn from one another! Multiculturalism is thus an artificial substitute for real cultural diversity. Slobodan Milosevic comes to mind once more: for years he stirred up political chaos in eastern Europe because of his passionate drive to create a monocultural Serbia, a unitary state where birds of a feather could flock together under the banner of all for one and one for all. This isn't universalism, it's fascism: the former Soviet Union, for instance, even though politically monolithic, was amazingly multicultural, an explosive mix, as current events in Chechnya, Dagestan, and elsewhere testify.

In the fall of 1998, there was an exhibition at the Minneapolis Institute of Arts which revealed postmodernism in full flower. The presentation was premised on an anti-hierarchical conception of the cultural realm: since according to postmodernist conceit, all cultures are allegedly co-equal, so are all art objects. As Carol Wintermute intimates, cultural studies tend nowadays to trump aesthetic analysis. Artistic individuality is deliberately downplayed, one is merely a product of the culture. Thus, at the exhibition a Mondrian painting was paired with art works completely unrelated: incoherence is not only taken for granted as reality's leitmotiv, it is to be celebrated eclectically, which merely betrays the rootlessness of our time. But is not the ability to distinguish one thing from another the animating characteristic of intelligence? What's going on—with postmodernism making common cause here with multiculturalism—is a false egalitarianism that mocks both intellect and differential individuality.

So I return to where I started: affirmation of the oneness of humanity encompassing a multidimensionality of communities and individuals. As modern art aspires to confirm the objectively shareable and the universally communicable in human experience, so does the American democratic ethos in the social, political and international arenas.

The UN Charter, a universal text, respects national sovereignty but not as a cover for a nation's brutal repression of its own people. If humanism stands firmly against all absolutisms, it must take an unequivocal position against the notion that national cultures can be forever legitimized in the name of an untouchable sovereignty. Unfettered cultural relativism, which supports such a point of view, cannot be permitted to serve as a mask for the crushing of individual human rights. In short, no political state owns its citizenry and has an inalienable right to do with it as it pleases. This applies as much to the United States as it does to China, Yugoslavia, or Singapore. The spirit of universalism, of the sacredness of the human individual, is amply embedded in international law in the 1945 Nuremberg Trials of Nazis who committed crimes against humanity, in the 1948 Universal Declaration of Human Rights and Convention Against Genocide, and in the UN's International War Crimes Tribunal (created in the aftermath of genocides in Rwanda and Bosnia), which in May of 1999 announced its indictment of Slobodan Milosevic for mass atrocities and deportations of innocent civilians carried out under his command in Kosovo. This action makes him subject to an international arrest warrant should he choose to flee Serbia and become, like Pinochet, an international pariah in danger of being apprehended wherever he goes.

A human rights tradition, which in the modern period stems pre-eminently from the Enlightenment, rests upon the spiritual value of every person's infinite worth. Once the contrary is accepted, that the sacred character and dignity of any person can be cavalierly denied, dehumanization cannot be far behind. The ideal envisioned here is a spiritually grounded humanist universalism which goes deeper than any multiculturalism through dialogic and behavioral interaction in pursuit of common ethical ground among the diversity of religious and secular philosophic traditions. Given human diversity, a global monoculture based largely on a market-oriented mentality is simply unachievable. Prior to all theologies, ideologies and philosophies is ethics: our first experience on earth is the experience of having to relate to one another, from the personal level onward. Ultimately we either connect or we die. Let us recall *Humanist Manifesto I's* vision: "The goal of humanism is a free and *universal* [italics mine] society in which people voluntarily and intelligently cooperate for the common good." Such iteration is born of the human quest for freedom and its natural corollary, human dignity.

Author's Philosophic Note

Lest there be any misunderstandings: references throughout this paper to universals has nothing whatever to do with Platonic realism, the metaphysical notion of pre-existing archetypes that subsist eternally before their imperfect empirical embodiment in time and space. Historical specificity is that from which the universalism espoused here has been drawn. Universals, as mentioned in regard to the two World Parliaments of Religion, are but a spiritual reprise of the underlining premises of the American Enlightenment.

As for NATO's seventy-eight-day air attack against the Serbs, it has to be accounted for as history's first explicitly humanitarian war: in a postmodern world paradoxes abound. The imperfect moral and political working hypothesis—owing to the unimaginable difficulty of applying the rule of law to issues of war and peace—appears to be a selective situational interventionism. At the moment, at least, that's the way things are—let us stay tuned.

9

MULTICULTURALISM—
YES, NO, MAYBE

Robert B. Tapp

Much current support for "multiculturalism" grounds in postmodern perspectives which so stress a relativistic stance that serious historical analysis becomes difficult. I will try here to untangle some of the historical ignorances and omissions that have served to polarize inquiry. Discussions are further complicated by terms—nation, civilization, ethnic group, race, culture, diversity, pluralism—which carry semantic ambiguity as well as discursive potency.

It will also become clear that what may be necessary or wise for a large society may be quite unwise within any group of significant others within that society. Certainly humanist groups continually face such questions as whether to define themselves narrowly and exclude others who may also claim to be humanists. In recent years, arguments among "secular" and "religious" humanists illustrate this. Persons in both camps probably feel that the "other" has a right to exist so long as it does not attempt to preempt the humanist label. Some have proposed describing humanism as a world-view or a lifestance to bridge this particular gap.

In the abstract we are dealing with an "us versus them" issue. More concretely, we can be widely understood if we notice the possible existence of several cultures within a nation, and perhaps several nations within a civilization. Dropping down in levels, we can speak of groups within a culture as well, of course, of individuals within groups. In actual fact, there are almost infinite permutations. The differentiations can stem from "race," ethnicity, sex, gender, class, religion, caste, sexual orientation, color, habitation, education—in all of their possible overlaps. (It hardly matters that UNESCO long ago established the biological meaninglessness of "race"). Nor does it matter that some groups are labeled "ethnic," since that term either applies to any and everyone or it has no useful meaning for classifying purposes.

Problems for Contemporary "Multiculturalists"

Many multiculturalists treat cultures as discrete and unchanging entities. But all cultures have histories, which means that they are continually changing. This is especially true in open and mobile societies such as the United States. Think of Andrew Greeley's wry observation that his fellow Irish had just ceased being an ethnic group as this status was coming into fashion (or his perceptive provocation that intellectuals were an ethnic group). Yes, there are still St. Patrick's Day parades, but in recent years these have faced their own recognition/identity problems, with gay and lesbian participants. A great deal of cultural change follows the pattern of Hansen's Law (known to many via Will Herberg) where first-generation immigrants cling together and to the old ways; their children reject all this in embracing Americanism; and the grandchildren return to some form of ethnicity as more supportive than simple American identity. I say "some form" because many cultural features that clung to the grandparents had been dropped by that third generation

Compounded by a few more generations plus ethnic intermarriage rates (using that term as the most neutral group descriptor), the situation becomes hopelessly muddied. Tiger Woods becomes a better prototype for the next century. Michael Lind writes of an America "beige" and "black."[1]

In my own personal case (hardly atypical), my father climbed out of a lower-class Irish (and Catholic) home to cross a railroad track and marry the upper-class German woman and convert to her Lutheranism. On St. Pat's day, should I wear green or orange? What should my Jewish grandchildren wear? And how about my non-Jewish grandchildren? Where do my Catholic nieces and nephews fit in? Or since I remarried, how does all this affect my Latino nephews and nieces?

There are various ways to treat ethnicity. Morris Raphael's English version, widely seen in the BBC production "Those Glittering Prizes," was to have the young Jewish student who has won entrance to Cambridge in the years before World War II reject his Orthodox father's criticism for adopting the ways of a gentile world, jump up from the table, and say that the only way to deal with a tradition is "to turn your back on it!"

A softer version appeared recently by Rosario Ferré:

Puerto Ricans living on the mainland think of the island in much the same way as African Americans think of Africa—as an almost mythical place inhabited by ancestral gods. For those Puerto Ricans, the homeland is a place of origin, proof of a vital "difference" that sets them apart from what can seem the vast sameness of the United States.

Puerto Ricans have been Americans since 1898, and our culture and language remain as healthy as ever. We are no longer poor, undernourished or anemic. We are mulatto-mestizo, bilingual and proud of it. We no longer need fear that "el otro," the other, will swallow us up.

We have become the other. As a Puerto Rican and an American, I believe our future as a community is inseparable from our culture and language, but I'm also passionately committed to the modern world. That's why I'm going to support statehood in the next plebiscite.[2]

Yet another version of dealing with ethnicity (more congenial to me) comes from the pianist/author Alfred Brendel in a recent interview:

I don't remember what Kundera wrote precisely, but my thoughts are these. I enjoy being positioned in the middle of things. I like to imagine that my family absorbed different traits: Austrian, German, Italian and Slav. I like the idea of federations; they don't always work, but that is no argument against them. Much of the great music I value comes from Central Europe. And there was a literary culture in Austria, epitomized by Robert Musil, the taking-in of which was a great influence in my 1920s. I dislike any kind of nationalism or regionalism. I do not feel the need to "belong." I have lived in London and felt cosmopolitan for nearly thirty years. Wherever I am, I prefer to be a paying guest.[3]

Take the simple proposition: All cultures in a pluralistic society deserve respect. Easy to accede until we think of the hard cases. Should some of our neighbors, for cultural reasons, insist on their right to deny medical treatment to their sick children? Should other groups insist that the public schools avoid sex education (because of their beliefs rather than any evidence of its alleged harmfulness)? What about cultures that practice infant genital alterations? While the male circumcision issue is still medically somewhat ambiguous, female infibulation has no known health merits and clear demerits. How much formal education should a state require of its youth? Should this standard be lowered to meet the practices of local cultures? The list of such conflicts grows as U.S. society becomes more diverse. The racist immigration laws have been changed and our military interventions outside our borders predictably generate refugee-immigrants.

Many U.S. cultures are impacted by law in terms of their customs and practices. Marriageable age, polygamy, sacrifice of animals, hallucinogen usages, hats and shawls and hair-stylings, uses as well as avoidances of violence, religious observances and practices, knowledge restrictions (health biology, evolution, history, linguistic patterns) quickly come to mind.

These intra-culture changes are not only a result of direct and restrictive outside influences. They can come as competitive countermeasures. Examples of this might be Kwanzaa, heightening the importance of Hanukkah, anti-Columbus Day celebrations.

The point here is simple and should be obvious—cultures in free society are very fluid structures. One generation's central focus may be marginalized by the next generation. Some practices may only remain as materials for satire, no doubt appropriate within the group but nevertheless an ambivalently-distancing device from the cultural past. One thinks of Yiddishisms, Sven and Ole jokes, Black English among bilingual African-Americans, Irish old sod stories.

Given these examples, it becomes clear that any agenda positing a relativistic equality of all cultures and therefore demanding equal respect for all raises some major problems. Just which historical moment of a culture it is that should be respected—now loses specificity. Moreover it fails to take account of intercultural impacts. Each of us, and the cultures that we reference, are surrounded by forces of "otherness," many of them quite real and some more imagined ("virtual," in today's jargon). Some of these othernesses are more palatable than others. Dare I instance the enormous appetite Americans have shown in recent years to sample each other's cuisines? What once only existed in large cities now can be found in small-town groceries. Or think in terms of music. How field shouts and chants, rooted in African homelands, birthed the blues and jazz, and then, with a change in pigmentation, became rock and roll. TIME magazine has even argued that the present reality of American music is hip-hop.[4]

These discussions of multiculturalism would be more realistic and more useful is they were better rooted historically. While a standard criticism is that American culture tries to integrate everyone into a "Eurocentric" mold, it is clear that from the earliest days, American thinkers saw themselves as building a new society, quite separate from that Europe that they had left. To speak simply of "the Enlightenment project," without seeing the real transformations intended by Jefferson, Madison, Franklin and many others, simply won't do. There was indeed an "American Enlightenment," given to practice and not just theory. Many European roots of those ideas were acknowledged, but the changed political structures and class distinctions made for fuller and different exercise.

America as Exception?

Let's now look more carefully at what critics call "the myth of American exceptionalism." Flaws are easy to find in the various records of political organizations that humans have tried. What makes the American experiment worthy of a second look? One of our leading historians who has also played larger political roles than most academics is Arthur Schlesinger Jr. He makes the following case for exceptionalism:

> The contemporary sanctification of the group threatens the old idea of a coherent society. Multicultural zealots reject as hegemonic the notion of a shared commitment to common ideals. How far the discourse has come from Crevecoeur's "new race," from Tocqueville's civic participation, from Emerson's "smelting pot," from Bryce's "amazing solvent," from Myrdal's "American Creed."
>
> Yet what has held the American people together in the absence of a common ethnic origin has been precisely a common adherence to ideals of democracy and human rights that, too often transgressed in practice, forever goad us to narrow the gap between practice and principles.[5]

The references here are clearly to the Enlightenment background of U.S. nationalism, where the clear note was a rejection of past forms of governing, political and ecclesiastical. None could be trusted, and power was therefore to be vested in the citizenry (i.e. the male, non-slave, and economically secure parts of that citizenry). Of course such individuals had "interests," but separating and spreading power would mitigate the harms that clashes of interest would bring. For this initial elite there was an implicit assumption that "knowledge was power," and that the relatively new sciences—embodying both reason and common sense—would expand human knowledge.

By the nineteenth century, political and economic problems abroad had brought waves of immigrants to U.S. shores. The young industrial society, having surmounted a devastating civil war, was eager for workers. And for the more restless, there was always that frontier, enlarged by wars and diplomacy. A new dialectic emerged between those who feared these new cultural and religious infusions and those who took their comfort in the expectation that the new public education system would integrate this new citizenry.

At the extreme were the Know Nothings who insisted on freezing their already-outdated image of a WASP society, and eliminating all deviations. The naivete of such a position renders it unstable and untenable—subject to periodic ridicule. Shortly after his 1933 inauguration, Franklin Roosevelt accepted a quite pro forma invitation to address the conservative and chauvinistic Daughters of the American Revolution. He began, "Fellow immigrants...."

Occupying a more middle ground were those who kept the rhetoric of the "new race" but more privately saw it as the extension of their own selves. Since those selves were continually being reshaped by their cultural contexts, it too afforded no firm grounding. More realistic was Randolph Bourne's descriptor of "cultural pluralism," a recognition of the perpetual changing that characterized an immigrant society.

Horace Kallen and John Dewey quickly built on this concept. In Dewey's philosophy, the simplistic view of an America into which the new immigrant would be integrated was transformed into a recognition of the historicity of cultures and the processes by which U.S. culture might be continually transformed into a culture based on ongoing knowledge from the sciences. Dewey, of course, was not a positivist, and his "science" included experiential social sciences. The transactions between organisms and their environments constituted culture and, for Dewey, culture was in continual change. The serious differentiation was between those cultures mistakenly thinking that they could remain static and those that accepted change and tried to insert intelligence into the process.

Here we would do well to speak of a U.S. "civilization" interacting with, transforming, and being transformed by the various "cultures" of the citizenry. Disputes among these cultures would not be resolved on the basis of priority but in terms of which alternative would have preferable outcomes for the civilization which all disputants inhabited. Such disputes necessitate an inquiry into the claims of all parties. In most cases, the outcomes will preserve some elements of all components. Each "resolution," in turn will at some future time be challenged by newcomers, and the rational evaluation will recommence.

Hmong migrants, in the early days of their Minnesota immigration, for instance, were hauled into court for netting songbirds for food. Minnesotans preferred eating larger birds, a preference which made no particular sense to their new neighbors. Existing laws should have been viewed as the occasion to resolve such a dispute rationally. Instead they were viewed as automatic arbiters. In other words, challenges always raise the issue of custom versus intelligent rule. If more Minnesotans had come from northern Italy, where until very recently small birds (uccelli) were netted and relished, the courts might have ruled differently.

It is where more serious issue clash that we need a more supple theoretical framework. Free expression is a good example. One community's literature might be seen by some other community as pornography. So far, the best solution has been to maximize freedom unless and until a "clear and present danger" from such expression can be demonstrated. The abortion issue, however, underscores both the obduracy of intergroup disputes as well as their shifting vectors. The emergence of a Religious Right in the United States suddenly brought a Protestant support to what had been a basically non-political issue for Roman Catholics. The emergence of homosexual rights movements created oppositions within traditional U.S. religions.

The Religious Factor

In our generalizations about conflicts among cultures and groups, we must recognize the paradigmatic role of religious absolutisms. Those who feel they possess the "truth" about a matter have no interest in hearing other positions. In the pre-Vatican II position of Roman Catholicism, "error does not have equal rights with truth." In my Los Angeles graduate student days in the 1940s, I led "reconciliation tours" (sponsored by the YM-YWCA) which gave Protestant highschoolers a chance to visit varieties of Buddhist, Hindu, and Catholic sites. At one of the latter, a student asked the friendly priest if it would not be a good idea for his youth to have similar tours. "What for?" was the abrupt answer—correct at that time, if not exactly polite.

Globalization may have the effect of relativizing that kind of absolutism for some, but it also can intensify it. To stay with the religious sphere, the intense world missionary activities of Euroamerican Protestants in the nineteenth century led to a World Missionary Conference in 1910 which aimed to reduce competitions among national groups. Uniting the "us" did nothing to include the "them." At a follow up meeting in 1928, the "them" was broadened to include those committed to "secularism." The next meeting in 1937 returned to Christian triumphalism.

Another lesson from history of religions, described by Peter Berger, is the tendency of variant Christian groups to band together when they are all weak (ecumenism) and then to compete when they are again strong.

This tension between ingroup solidarity and multigroup tolerance looms large at the end of the twentieth century. The forces of imperialism (Euroamerican and Russian) have weakened at the end of the Cold War, and the intergroup "peace" they imposed in their areas can no longer override ethnic hostilities. Ireland, Yugoslavia, India, Indonesia, Southeast Asia, Africa have all been plagued by forms of ethnic cleansing (the Friends Committee on National Legislation is quite right to refuse this euphemism, however ironic it might seem, and to call them "purges). Note the deep religious rootages of most of these conflicts: Christian/Muslim, Catholic/Orthodox, Hindu/Muslim, Muslim/Buddhist. In tribal cultures, the essence of the tribe is religious.

To some extent, of course, there may be underlying factors in these conflicts: economic, political, regional. A recent *New York Times* lead editorial tries to recover this high ground for the religions:

> Some have characterized the war in the Balkans as an ancient implacable conflict among religions. But in fact, it is testimony to the ability of ruthless leaders to persecute others in the name of religion, ignoring the genuine tradition of tolerance enshrined in Judaism, Christianity and Islam and articulated by the prophets, saints and seers of each faith. In a season when adherents to these great religions are worshiping God in their own ways, it is especially important to remember the horrors of viewing others with different backgrounds as strangers, or even enemies, whether they live in Northern Ireland, the Balkans, the Middle East, Indonesia or any other place of entrenched religious and ethnic conflict. Thus this season's confluence of holidays and horrors can serve as a powerful reminder of that higher yearning among peoples of all traditions.[6]

"Higher yearning" may be a useful phrase, but what is really at stake is ethical ambiguity; the tension between "My country right or wrong" and "What is really right on some universal basis higher than nationalism." While most religions contain that latter injunction, it is seldom operative. More fruitful is the distinction between "official" religion and "popular" religion. The official religion may exist in texts and even occasionally in clerics, but the popular religion typically predominates. Should we attend to the scholars or the pollsters, and in what proportions? Humanists have traditionally stressed the importance of actual and operative ethics. To ignore the actual while insisting upon some theoretical makes for poor judgments.

In many part of Europe, social freedom and economic improvements have seen a decline in formal religions. This has not been so true in the former Soviet empire and is certainly not the case in the United States. What is important is the set of new values embraced, whether within some religion or apart from it. Salman Rushdie puts this well:

> By agreeing on what we are against, we discover what we are for. Andre Malraux believed that the third millennium must be the age of religion. I would say rather that it must be the age in which we finally grow out of our need for religion. But to cease to believe in our gods is not the same thing as commencing to believe in nothing.[7]

A Humanist Perspective

Given the instance of intergroup tensions, what are the best strategies for democratic societies? Foremost, it seems to me, is the establishment of legal systems based on the recognition of universal human rights. Along with this must come a reduction of the economic underpinnings of tension. Once "green families" have the same income range as "purple families," much of the tension will disappear. None of this can realistically occur without the overarching oversight of an international community dedicated to pluralism.

These key aspects of a humanistic perspective assume and require the education of individuals based upon the free flow of information. How ironic that the Internet, developed initially for military purposes, now fosters free information flows. Humanists have always assumed that informed peoples will struggle for their freedoms. We need to emphasize that informed people will also have better understanding of their neighbors and therefore be less likely to stereotype them or to "buy into" distortions.

Humanists have historically been meliorists, not utopians. That is, they have always sought ways to improve their culture's status quo, without ever assuming that this task of improvement would end in some kind of perfect society. Dewey's eternal problem-solving comes to mind—the search for ways toward ends-in-view, the implementation of present values, the contrast between dream and reality (to revert to Gunnar Myrdal's useful distinction). This restlessness, this drive to make things better stems from the nontheism of the humanists. This is not the best of all possible worlds because it was created by some perfect divinity. Nor is it a world where some divinity will, in time, make things better. The evolution of human intelligence puts the potency for improvement, as well as the responsibility, solely in human hands.

Multiculturalism versus Pluralism

Let me now expand on the connotations of contemporary multiculturalism. As cultural theorists use the term, it connotes a relativism. Or rather, it extends the relativism assumed by postmodern discourse: since no construct is grounded or rests on any fundamentals, all constructs are equally arbitrary. On this basis, there is no arguable reason for preferring one culture to another. More importantly, it follows that there is no justifiable basis for criticizing any aspect of any culture since this would have to be done from some other equally relative cultural standpoint. In the hands of some recent educationists, this has generated a self-esteem curriculum where student problems are traced to a lack of positive cultural identity. Somehow, the histories of all cultures must be shown as equally meritorious.

Critics have been many on this issue. Richard Bernstein suggests that such relativism is a fraud "perpetuated by mostly middle-class intellectuals, all of whom have jobs."[8] The change in climate, he argues, stems not from any increase in U.S. diversity but from "our unwillingness to see the American identity as worthy enough to expect newcomers to adopt it as their own."[9] In his two years preparing this book, Bernstein says "I have rarely met a multiculturalist ideologue who bothered to learn anything beyond a few heartwarming cliches about another culture, or even evinced much curiosity about a people other than his own."[10]

He accused them of purveying a watered-down and re-sloganed Marxism, and calls upon

> liberals to recapture the high ground from the demagogues of diversity, to declare their diversity fake, fraudulent, superstitious, cranky, sanctimonious, monotonous. It is time to reaffirm the greatest engine of genuine diversity that the world has ever known, which is the liberal-democratic society sustained by a set of concepts now dismissed as the narratives of the people in charge."[11]

The African-American Situation

Much of the discussion of multiculturalism is complicated by the situation of African Americans, descendants of slaves who were forced migrants and not eager immigrants to the "New World." Their purchasers broke up family structures, language groups, religious groups, and all else that threatened to preserve something of human dignity. The Civil War was but a momentary surcease in this systematic human degradation. Once the slaves were allowed to be converted to Christianity, a serious racism had emerged to support the continuance of this degradation and separatism.[12] In 1815, Emerson had included "Africans and Polynesians" in his "smelting pot," but this brief moment was largely ignored. African Americans were essentially ignored by promoters of Americanization and assimilation in the later nineteenth century. Various "back to Africa" stirrings found wide endorsements by other Americans. The National Association for the Advancement of Colored People, after all, was only founded in the early twentieth century.

Admittedly, "race" was a widely used construct in the past century. Even the Irish were viewed as a race (and a troublesome and inferior one). But the social control of African Americans proved lasting and obdurate. (The forced relocation of Nisei [Japanese Americans] in World War II was a tragic mixture of hysteria, ignorance, greed, and a modified racism—since other Asian citizens were not so stigmatized). Only Native Americans have been subjected to a similarly long-lived stigmatization by law and custom. Where the other Americans permitted themselves a limited romanticization of "Indians," this was seldom extended to African Americans. Demeaning stereotypes were standard. One would never learn from the Hollywood film output of World War II that the U.S. Armed Forces were rigidly segregated.

I was vice-chair of the Los Angeles County Commission on Human Relations in that postwar period, and our agenda focused heavily on the particular problems of the African-American population and the incredible resistance by most other Americans to see or meliorate this chain of injustices. One of our major thrusts was to get the City Council to pass a fair employment ordinance. The existence of a second pressure group made it easier for the Council to stall. That second group was spearheaded by the Communist Party and the few remaining labor unions that it controlled. In view of the failure of those in that second group to support racial integration or oppose Japanese-American relocation during the war period, my group carefully but firmly rejected those who formed that second group. I mention this to remind younger readers of the ideological chasms during that period.

Nathan Glazer, Harvard University expert on ethnicity, has written a poignant book summing up his distinguished career entitled *We Are All Multiculturalists Now*.[13] The title is ironic, and reflects a deep despair. He looks out at the "culture wars" surrounding the multicultural issue and mourns that these

> reflect a hard reality that none of us wants, that all of us want to see disappear, but that none of us knows how to overcome. it is only change in that larger reality that will reduce multiculturalism to a passing phase in the complex history of the making of an American nation from many strands.[14]

He is probably correct in seeing present U.S. identity politics as monopolized by an African-American agenda, and that this may be regrettable even though understandable. In terms of most curricular materials, this leaves out various Hispanic groups as well as South Asians, Southeast Asians [here the labeling becomes absurd, but "pan-Asian" is equally unacceptable], Africans [an equally absurd umbrella], Native American [same problem], Pacific Islanders.... Serious awareness of all these groups is curricularly unachievable. They became parts of U.S. life for many disparate reasons. Certainly the Nicaraguans who fled the Sandinistas and those who fled Reagan's "Contras" have little in common beyond language. The Vietnamese of the United who were fortunate enough to be airlifted when their cause failed are certainly different from the Vietnamese of Chinese descent who were driven out by the victors.

Multiculturalism likewise rests upon the untenable assumption that culture is a stable entity. How to view the "old country" is a function of many new factors—why one left, inherited and imputed class status, educational/professional achievement and their transferability, regionalism, how readily assimilation is available, cultural intermarriage, religious conversions, upward mobility, American caste structures. For all these reasons, assigning any stable "culture" label on individuals is highly problematic.[15]

The pluralism construct serves us much better. It recognizes not only variety but change, not only difference but similarity. John Hume, the Nobel Peace laureate of northern Ireland put this well "Difference is an accident of birth; difference is the essence of humanity."[16] Consider again that basic humanist principle that we are all better served in society when all of us can contribute most fully. Humans should be wanted (family planning), nurtured (emotional supports), intellectually fulfilled (education), permitted to contribute (employment), permitted to flourish (health, social stability, play, pleasure).

When these basic human rights are recognized and implemented, irrational discriminations (those based on sex, gender, "race," belief, sexual preference, class) will lose much of their force. Instead, individuals will freely explore possibilities of achievement throughout the whole life cycle, learning from each other and contributing to each other. Lest this sound utopian, we need to remind ourselves that the discovering of nature (including human natures) is an ever-expanding process—one where each solution opens new problems for us.

Marx was brilliant in showing the ways that trivial distinctions between groups obscure the more serious divisions. He was also brilliant in showing ways that incorrectly identifying one's group led to false consciousness. But any simplistic distinction between

bourgeois and proletarian has little use today in the mixed econo-
mies that dominate developed countries. What are the real issues in
our time? Try justice. We are not yet able to relate equal rights to
equal incomes or wealth. We have here a genuine and unresolved
pluralism. Perhaps overarching this is an ideological/ethical division
that ran through the Cold War and recently resurfaced in the flap
over an Academy award to Elia Kazan. If he, under oath, named
names—was he a "rat," a "patriot," or a newly-rehabilitated "liberal?" One group of absolutists among us saw/see the Communist
Party as a political party among parties (Kazan was a "rat"). Another group of absolutists, claiming to own something they call
"Americanism," view Kazan as an ex-traitor. A more nuanced view,
found on the liberal-left, viewed Kazan as saying the right thing at
the wrong time in the wrong arena. The American C.P. was never a
clear and present danger to the U.S. government, but it had acquired
at that time significant power in some labor unions and some segments of the film industry. And it had done so by using fronts (e.g
the Progressive Citizens of America and Henry Wallace), deception
(talking racial integration in the United States while rationalizing
ethnic preserves in the USSR), and subversion (no free speech for
Trotskyites, no wartime strikes). Sidney Hook, in the spirit of
Dewey, described the issues in this period of history well with his
slogan "Heresy, yes; conspiracy, no."[17]

Most of the things that present groups view as dividers are essentially involuntary—artifacts of birth and thus of chance—skin
color, sex, gender, class, nationality, ethnicity, religion, sexual preference. What should we be discussing when the divisions based on
these have been lessened by one level of pluralism? I have already
mentioned justice. Others might want ethics and the good to be
central. Yet others will want to underscore beauty, and others will
focus on the development of full personalities. Most of us, however, will agree that the shift to pluralistic societies engaging in such

important pursuits will require continual inquiry into the nature of nature and our natures. Thus the development of the sciences will be the necessary foundation of future societies, and the core of education for the young.

Not only do immigrant Americans face the problem of relationships to some "old country." Whenever that former country changes radically, these have to be reassessed. Think of U.S. "White Russians" after the fall of Russian communism. Or Iranian Americans after Khomeini's revolution. Or of Japanese Americans—interned during WW II, apologized to long after many had died.

Even greater problems arise, however, in the process of making more accurate assessment of key elements in the "shared" versions of U.S. history. Consider Christopher Columbus. Alleged memories of his places in Genoese, Portuguese, and Spanish history abound. Strong claims of his Jewish ancestry add to the puzzles. In recent years, however, he is being re-assessed as a cruel slaver, consumed by a kind of biblical fanaticism. As to his "discovery" of a New World—that claim only makes any sense from a European standpoint. Native Americans ("Indians") clearly have seen him as a cruel conqueror and bearer of disease and slavery. As our writing of history becomes less biased and more global, so does the way U.S. history is taught in the schools. And this, after all, is where memories are refashioned. And this process will accelerate as more groups become effectively enfranchised. University departments of women's studies, black studies, Chicano studies, gay studies, and their many counterparts will both insist upon and play major roles in unearthing those facts that will correct the historical memories.

Ours is a rather unique moment in human history. Globalization stretches around the planet with its message that some form of market economy is the best way to maximize the human potentials of a maximal number of persons. Even China's "marxists" seem moving in this direction. But unlimited free markets, especially where there are no democratic checks on the bottom-line mentalities of industrial managers and their financiers, produce ecological and human disasters. Salman Rushdie makes a telling argument against relativizing this situation:

> [A]re there other universals besides international conglomerates and the interests of superpowers? And if by chance there were a universal value that might, for the sake of argument, be called "freedom," whose enemies—tyranny, bigotry, intolerance, fanaticism—were the enemies of us all; and if this "freedom" were discovered to exist in greater quantity in the countries of the West than anywhere else on earth; and if, in the world as it actually exists, rather than in some unattainable Utopia, the authority of the United States were the best current guarantor of that "freedom," then might it not follow that to oppose the spread of American culture would be to take up arms against the wrong foe.[18]

The risk is that all the older polarizations will be replaced by a horrendous and bloody split between have and have-not. In the past, divisions over what we have been calling the involuntary distinctions of color, gender, sexual orientation, religion, and the like have obscured this other source of misery and human wastage. Our unique challenge is to use the power of globalization to overcome every kind of polarization. To obstruct one gender or ethnic group from achieving full human potential is to slow the development of any society. That particular case can be made rather readily in our epoch of serious social and economic data. We now need to devise an equally effective strategy to make it self-evident that dooming any bloc of humans to live in poverty, whatever the rationale, similarly destroys human development.

When humanists use words such as "full potential" and "human development" within the world group of cultures that we all inherit, we are clearly talking about radical changes that must be brought about in all of them. Whether we call this social progress or social evolution is a rhetorical choice. Humanists have committed to such radical change precisely because there are no inevitable cosmic directions (except perhaps entropy) and no plausible evidences of any cosmic helpers. Our best resource is critical intelligence—but not in the sense of some abstruse rationality. Rather we must critically consider all the values that humans have cherished thus far in our trajectory on this planet. The criteria? Whether they bring more humans into their own potentials and thus move us toward a true world community. Any multiculturalism that sees all cultures as equally valid would freeze an untenable status quo. A critical multiculturalism will call upon every culture to promote those values that enhance human development and to outgrow those that impede.

Pluralism within Humanist Groups

If humanist groups are to play their proper role in leading toward world societies with these goals, they will need to think carefully about the clues to their own effectiveness. Clearly the involuntary forms of social division have no place in humanist groups, and inclusiveness must be the basis. This will make realistic a healthy pluralism in which varied points of view are known both at first and second hand. In other words, humanists need to be, in principle, color-blind but in practice keenly sensitive to the human damage that focus on color has meant. So too with gender, class, sexual preference, religion, and the other divisions based upon accidents of birth.

But our philosophies and ideologies are not lifelong accidents of birth. We need consciously to adopt these, even those of us who were fortunate to be born into humanistic climates. Put another way, these are too important to have been left to the choices of our parents (whom we did not choose). Humanists need to be very clear about the roles religions and ideologies have played in human history. They need to devise therapies for themselves and others who come out of repressive and anti-human systems. But their focus needs to be on humanist authenticity so that the commitments and stances of their groups are there for all to see.

In this sense, a multicultural humanist group is an anomaly. An early Christian church father said that "Lips that praise Jahweh cannot praise Jupiter." Humanists must remain clear that praise of the supernaturals denigrates the human. Goddesses are no better than gods, and religious tradition X probably has the same poor track record as religious tradition Y. Arthur Clarke in Childhood's End suggests a future scene in which superior beings dominate belligerent humans and give them a television-like device that can be tuned to any past time and place. Overnight, the religions, with all their historical falsifications, disappear. Only a form of Buddhism survived.

A more humanist version of this narrative would begin with threads in India, China, and Greece that saw humans as a part of the natural world (and not dominators or victims). This narrative would recognize us as embodied, as experiencing both pleasures and pains, and as gifted with visions and dreams to improve the situations in which we found ourselves. We are not lost citizens of some unearthly realm, waiting to return. Instead we are that part of nature which has not only become conscious but has visioned the possibilities and responsibilities for changing and improving both ourselves and the surrounding world. Pain and disease are not punishments from the gods but aspects of nature needing improvement. Birth is the chance to flourish rather than the curse of entering an evil world. Death is not release and transport to some other realm but the natural end of all living things—a cosmic recycling. And life therein is a truly sacred realm, where the human can flourish, can dream, create, know, experience.

Against some of the postmodern critics, ours is a universal, even foundational, view. A view building upon evolution, changes that are adaptive and that also change the environments in which adaptation occurs. Humans are too insignificant a part of the universe for us to claim that there is any overall purpose running through energy/matter. Yet we are that part of existence where purposing can occur. The philosophies of the world's humanists, ancient as well as modern, concur that this purposing is the very essence of life, and that purposes guided by wisdom are the meaning of life.

In a profound sense, humanists have become "cosmopolitans"[19] by their very commitment to reason and the possibility of knowledge. This leads them to take the sciences seriously and to take ethics seriously. That same commitment shows them that human liberation demands the transcending of historical ethnicities and religiosities.

Humanist groups must therefore be inclusive since no group has a monopoly of skill or knowledge. They must be pluralistic since a number of lifestyles have succeeded in promoting life. But they must embody a critical intelligence which knows that not all cultures are equal or the same; a critical intelligence which refines the capacities to make careful selections from all cultures and wise choices among them.

Notes

1. Michael Lind, "The Beige and the Black," *New York Times Magazine* (Aug. 16, 1998).

2. Op-Ed., *New York Times* (March 19, 1999).

3. Interview with Johanna Keller, *New York Times* (April 4, 1999).

4. *TIME*, passim.

5. Arthur M. Schlesinger Jr., *The Disuniting of America: Reflections on a Multicultural Society* (New York: Norton, 1998), p. 123.

6. *New York Times* (April 4, 1999).

7. *New York Times* (March 5, 1999).

8. Richard Bernstein, *Dictatorship of Virtue: Multiculturalism and the Battle for America's Future* (New York: Knopf, 1994), p. 10.

9. Ibid., p. 154.

10. Ibid., p. 213.

11. Ibid., p. 346.

12. Cf. Buell Gallagher, *Color and Conscience, the Irrepressible Conflict* (New York: Harper & Bros., 1946).

13. Nathan Glazer, *We Are All Multiculturalists Now* (Cambridge: Harvard University Press, 1997).

14. Ibid., p. 161.

15. These barriers, to be sure, vary from one ethnicity to another, especially in the case of African-Americans.

16. C-Span, Jan. 18, 1999. Speech during Atlanta celebration for Martin Luther King, Jr.

17. Sidney Hook, *Heresy, Yes—Conspiracy, No* (New York: John Day, 1953).

18. Loc. cit.

19. Stalin, quite correctly, saw those who had such a cosmopolitan commitment as the enemies of his totalitarian pseudo-science. He was only wrong in thinking that most cosmopolitans were Jews

and that therefore most Jews were cosmopolitans. This faulty logic only exacerbated his anti-Semitism.

10

A GLOBAL ETHIC IN A VARIOUS WORLD[*]

Howard Radest

Moral Experience

Experience sets the problems to which moral ideas respond. Too often, however, ethics is approached sub specie eternitatis as if, following Spinoza, it can be a discipline like mathematics. Or, inspired by Plato on the one hand and Kant on the other, we look for ethics in the worlds of reason. Failing that, we turn to natural law or history—to Aristotle or St. Thomas or Hegel and their embodiments in virtue theory or Marxism. Sometimes, we presume that ethics can be modeled on the notions of discovery and verification found in the sciences. Inspired by feminism, we turn to an ethics of care, building on the paradigmatic relationship of mother and child.

[*] An earlier version of this paper was presented at Kyung Hee University, Seoul, Korea, September, 1995 in honor of the 50th Anniversary of the United Nations.

Finally, skeptical of the moral enterprise itself, we surrender to emotivism, intuitionism, and nihilism.

But, I am a pragmatist and pragmatism is a welcoming philosophy. So, I am not discouraged by variety. Besides, each try at ethics is a response to experience too, even where reference to experience is suppressed. Today, a new experience is in the making so we may expect even more variousness in ethics. We need to make moral sense across the divides of concept, class, gender, race, nation, and culture in a global setting. We can't legislate values from within or on behalf of any particular idea-world or life-world. An abstract universalism will not do either. A global ethic demands an encounter with the "doings and sufferings" of an inclusive humanity and that defeats the simplicities of the past.

I am tempted to remain mute. Foolishly, however, I do not! I thought at first to begin with human "needs" and to see how a global ethic might respond to them. That seemed sensible enough since we are surely psycho-biological entities with commonalities that transcend biography, location, and time. But that either says very little or else claims too much. "Needs" are culturally and socially constructed from the outset by language and custom. Thus, a typically Western approach to "needs" centers values in the person and not in collectivity, in a timeless present and not in history, and in biology rather than spirit. Such an ethic would not accord with the practices, habits, and perceptions of human beings in many parts of the world where tribe and clan, tradition and ancestry, are ontologically and morally prior. That I may not find such views hospitable is beside the point. The task is a globally usable ethics and not a parochial one.

I am quite likely to see my own needs—even if unwittingly—as everyone's, to legislate out of myself what ought and ought not be. That is tempting too, the Emersonian trap that assimilates soul and over-soul, that connects everyone to everything. So, another trial. I turn to the moral disasters of our age, e.g., holocaust, war, terror, in order to show how a global ethic might offer remedy. After all, even the post-modernist finds commonality in the commandment, do not hurt one another.[1] But, I realize how easy it is to move from this minimalism to "do no harm" and then to an intrusive moralism, and this apart from the question of what "harm" means under differing circumstances. Finally, I am warned of the dangers which a global ethic faces, above all the dangers of egoism and cultural arrogance.

It may be that a global ethics is a chimera and the effort not merely thankless but pointless. That would be a valuable lesson in humility, itself a step on some bare and naked road to virtue. I must keep it in mind as a background reality for what follows. But, I am not yet ready for the disheartening conclusion that all I can do is keep silent. For one, there are transnational and transcultural moral issues that can neither be ignored nor addressed from within nation and culture. So I face a global problem whether I like it or not and even if, at times, I conclude it has no solution

Thankfully, I do not come to a global ethic untutored by history. I recall centuries-long struggles to enhance human possibilities and overcome human limitations. I know that our age is not unique in its humanism. The Classics, the Renaissance, and the Enlightenment make their moral claim as do equivalent eras in Asia, Africa, Latin America. Building on what has gone before, our age takes seriously the search for peace without conquest, witnesses the effort at decent ways to resolve conflict, struggles for the recognition of persons who have been treated as non-persons, for the liberation of human powers through science, technology, and education, for the appreciation of the diverse personalities and cultures which make up the human race, for a just response to the needs of labor, of women, of the poor. Yet, our age *is* unique, I think, in that the globe itself is becoming self-conscious in ways never before possible. The moral agenda is attentive in new ways.

Still, I hesitate. The dream of one world may be illusion. But then the fact of one world is not. We have moved toward greater global inclusiveness of nations, persons, and communities, of races and classes. In part this is an outcome of science and technology, in part it is a response to an emerging web of political-economic relationships, and in part it is a function of moral expectation. But these developments are also bitter-sweet. One world chokes on its own waste, threatens a destructiveness dreamt of only in Armageddon, and invites exploitation on a scale that dwarfs all previous tyrannies. One world, then, is a confession of how much remains to be done at least as much as it is an achievement. A global ethic labels a possibility.

One world is compromised by violence and fragmented by parochialism. Universality has been the aim of conquerors from the *Pax Romana* to Lenin's world revolution and Hitler's "thousand year Reich." Religions and ideologies have tried to rule the globe using threats of damnation in the next world and holy war in this one. Whether in the guise of the political state or of the one true faith, one world is subverted by the belief that unity may be imposed by those who "know" they possess the true and the good. Those imposed upon are simply inferior or heretical or, at best, misguided. Conquest, crusade, and jihad are forms of a global ethic too. At the same time, international law, the law of nations, dating from the 16th century, evolves. In the decades since Nuremberg, it develops yet further in the debate between sovereignty and "crimes against humanity," most recently in the case of General Augusto Pinochet of Chile.[2]

Today, whether in Beijing or Tokyo, Lusaka or Marrakech, Brasilia or Washington or Paris, we challenge the notion that truth and right reside singularly in any one part of the human race or in any one part of the globe. Of course, this challenge has not been successful—not yet, perhaps never, certainly not in my lifetime. Ethnocentrism, nationalism, collective egoism, and spiritual arrogance are still very much with us. New threats appear too. Multinational corporations become centers of global power, nihilism expresses itself in terrorism, ideology becomes fanaticism.

Yet, a great shift is occurring. Everywhere voices are raised denying that conquest or exploitation is morally acceptable. This points to an unarticulated and widely shared moral intuition whose force should not be minimized. To be sure, it is rooted in the cosmopolitanism of the Enlightenment and to that extent comes to world history with a Western pedigree. But it is equally true that this intuition has found ready adherents in a diversity of cultural and social milieus.[3] There seems then something globally truthful in notions like liberty, equality, and solidarity. But, it would not do to over-interpret these metaphors. They stand for a radical move against the past and a promising move toward the future. But, as we know all too well, the "devil is in the details." So, these notions of the Enlightenment—and of its most recent incarnation, the Universal Declaration of Human Rights in 1948—initiate an inquiry.[4] They open up the moral question.

Some Requirements of a New Global Ethic

Authority

Even the most "realistic" of Machiavellians pretends to moral legitimacy. History records competing views of rightful power variously based in claims of ontological or moral or historical "truth." "Divine right" authorized the rule of kings and princes. "Might makes right" justified the ethics of conquest since "might," after all, was a sign—from on high, from history—of "right." The "moral superiority" of race, culture or nation justified imperialism; "national destiny" justified expansionism; faith justified the crusade. These habits of justification persist, e.g., economic imperialism becomes the morality of the free market; a politics of national interests is masked as a struggle for freedom.

Scope

If the ground for a global ethic is shifting, so too is its dimension. Of course, claims of faith and nation on one side and of universalism on the other are still in play. Each is, however, blind to the other; each is incomplete in its grasp of the world. By contrast, a global ethic must take account of two facts of experience: the fact of the diversity of peoples and communities and the fact that none of these can be isolated from the others. It is no longer possible, then, to get away with defining ethics from within a particular culture as in the notion that there are only "Greeks and barbarians." Similarly, it is unconvincing to deduce the moral law from a finite set of universal premises as did Kant and Spinoza. The moral project today is instructed by the double knowledge that we live on one earth but that at the same time we live within a crazy quilt of collectivities.

These collectivities cannot help but encounter each other. They are forced to acknowledge a common-world if only as an arena for conflict, conversion, and conquest. But an unmediated reality of winners and losers ultimately reduces to confrontations of power. At that point, we face a *third* fact. Given modern technologies, power moves toward the instability of terrorism. In the "cold war," we learned the doctrine of "mutually assured destruction," appropriately abbreviated as MAD. Today, the tools of terror are accessible to the gang with minimal resources. It is possible then to imagine a world in which everyone exercises a veto and no one achieves a positive end. Under such a condition paralysis becomes the best possible outcome. The realism of a global ethic becomes apparent.

A new global ethic then is to be defined by a dialectic between globalism and localism.[5] Of course, there will remain a few enclaves that will try to stay unconnected, tribal nations like Iraq and Afghanistan or nostalgic turns to an uncluttered past like the so-called cultural conservatives in the United States. Within such life-worlds, it is possible, for a while at least, to have a protected ethic that permeates the public and the private, the social and the personal, i.e., a totalitarian ethic. But even enclaves and nostalgias are infected by the modern.

Each of us comes to live in multiple life-worlds each of which has its own identity and function.[6] With that, each of us becomes a carrier of subversion. As communicative cultures evolve, we become masters of many languages, defenders of many values.[7] Persons are not then the anonymous ciphers of the 1950s, the "lonely crowd" or "mass man," but rather *multinonymous*. As multiple life-worlds become normative, ethics is fragmented into many substructures. Coherence is at best partial. Consequently, each life-world has its dissidents and their number increases. We become both supportive and subversive of the life-worlds we inhabit. These continue to function as "roots" and "sources" of identity, of life-style, but we find ourselves with multiple roots and sources—socially, politically, morally, aesthetically, religiously, etc. The issue is not "alienation" but transition.

The talk of cultural diversity, multiculturalism and the like does not capture this multiplicity of identities since it tends to focus on collective entities that think to isolate themselves from each other. But, we are moving into a situation of experienced multiple life-worlds. It is not surprising then that we are morally disoriented, that the passions of denial are so tempting. If the conservative tries to return to a coherent life-world—or at least to recreate its fantasy—the liberal tries to create a global life-world with a comprehensive ethic of its own, to do away with tribe and nation. Cosmopolitanism then is the complement of sectarianism and reflects the same prevalent escapism. While seeming to face in different directions, both conservative and liberal are moved by the impulse to evade the pains of transition. Of course, they do not succeed. A radical distinction between the scope, functions and style of a global and a local ethics appears.

It follows that a global ethic—indeed all ethics—is going to be partial. This opens the epistemological problem of moral coherence in a new way. It calls for a new moral logic, a harmonics of concordance and dissonance. Thus, a global ethic will attend to what affects us as a species. It will be indifferent to many goods and many evils, perhaps most goods and most evils. It will remain for life-worlds to specify the ultimate ends and qualities of life and living. This will, no doubt, be unsatisfying and frustrating. Since the Stoics, we have dreamed of a single moral state, a single and comprehensive moral truth. But that is not to be and indeed ought not to be. Those of us who expect a unified set of personal and public moral values are going to be disappointed.

Failure to respect the limits of a global ethic invites totalitarianism. The harsh fact is that the personal and communal choices of others, no matter what I may think of them, are not for me to dictate. I may demur, disagree, argue against, preach, pray, condemn, grow angry. But, save for explicitly articulated exceptions, I am not authorized to coerce. A global ethic that seeks to impose one best pattern—of course, my own pattern—would have to conceive itself as universal, superior, worthy of species-wide obedience and the like. But this is precisely what is denied by the democratic expectation. A global ethic sets obligatory standards for what touches us in common. It establishes borders and boundaries. Beyond that, it must remain silent.[8] On the other hand, once limited to its proper task, the chances of a global ethic being effective are increased.

Ends

Within my life-worlds, I preach the special mission of faith or culture. I may share these with strangers, perhaps in hope of converting them. But, they do not experience my life-worlds as I do; they are strangers and can refuse. Meanwhile, a widely shared secularity[9] exists alongside of and penetrates into just about all life-worlds. This shared secularity—what I would call the material life of the species—arises on the ground of science and technology, of economic and industrial development, of the transmission of goods and services. Once, we shared experience within life-worlds; now we also share experience both across and independently of life-worlds. We find ourselves within a complexity of experiences to which we are unaccustomed and for which we are untrained.

No life-world is insulated from the influences of the material life of the globe. Whatever awaits us in some heaven or hell or at the end of history, a demand for the benefits of earthly living is heard everywhere. The democratic expectation thus has its economics as well as its politics. So while we will, no doubt, continue to hold to ultimate and transfinite ends-in-view, an emerging worldliness sets the pattern for the species-world, for shared global practices. While not in opposition to faith and culture, these practices create the common setting within which life-worlds are to be accommodated and to which they must accommodate themselves. Of course, things change as life-worlds and species-world interact. But then, no matter their claims of eternity and permanence, life-worlds always did change. They cannot help but respond to the dynamics of their own structures, the need to meet new secular challenges, and the influences of other life-worlds.

A global ethic cannot claim divine or ideological sanction. Arising between persons and collectivities with diverse loyalties and values, it is located within the natural world. In that sense, therefore, it takes shape as a form of "contract," i.e., a mutual agreement in which expectation is acknowledged by participation, in which expectation is enabled. The end in view is quite modest, the achievement of respectful accommodation. This sets the stage for continuities and innovations within life-worlds, provides their assurance as it were, but does not itself aim at an ideal. Thus, secularity sustains the chance of enriched life-possibilities just because it guards against the attempt to dismiss life-worlds for species-world or the conversion of species-world into life-world. Respectful accommodation, thus, is not mere toleration. It is an activity undertaken for the sake of appreciations and represents a stance against a history of the universal claims of empire, faith, and ideology.

An Ethic of Rights

To account for a multiplicity of life-worlds and their interaction in a species-world, a global ethic must deal with boundary relationships. The first thing that comes to mind then is "keep out." Or, as Robert Frost reminds us, "good fences make good neighbors." It follows that an invitation is needed before I can legitimately cross a boundary. Of course, I also need to know who can rightfully issue an invitation and whether or not entry is ever permissible without invitation. This opens up notions like non-violation, privacy, self-determination and the like. But these generate their own moral problems. For example, the notion of "non-interference" as in the "self-determination" of nations or in Star Trek's "prime directive" would seem to leave us with little legitimate recourse when groups or nations engage in genocide. Further, boundaries are never clearly drawn in the actual world and boundary disputes are unavoidable. Life-worlds typically try to occupy moral or spiritual common spaces as well as the spaces of other life-worlds. The species-world too can become oppressive. Finally, individuality can turn into individualism and absolutize the personal boundary.

But, despite many difficulties, we do live in a world where an ethic of rights is at work. This may be read as a project that legitimates boundaries. It tells us that a global ethic will be deontological rather than eudaemonistic,[10] will work with processes rather than final ends. Intuitively, this fits with the idea that a global ethic must be non-invasive. That follows, once we grant the legitimacy of an individuation of persons, a multiplicity of life-worlds, and a diversity of traditions. It becomes impossible to describe *the substance* of the moral life except by means of comparative studies. And, it becomes impossible to prescribe *the content* of the moral life except locally, i.e., within a life-world or set of related life-worlds.

The scope of an ethic of rights is wide and shallow, wide in its extension to the species-world and shallow in its limitation to boundary conditions. Thus, we have opted for a justice ethic and denied ourselves a virtue ethic, i.e., a set of *prima facie* goods like courage or integrity. Virtues may be defined in a formal language but they acquire content only when embedded in a particular community and enacted by one or several paradigmatic moral characters. Similarly, we have denied ourselves an ethic of caring[11] which relies upon the actual encounter of persons, even if only the encounter of strangers or of imagined encounters yet to come.[12] These encounters are interpersonal. But a global ethic needs to apply beyond persons to relationships between collectives and to their agents. To be sure, these agents may exhibit certain functional virtues, e.g., the virtues summed up by "fiduciary responsibilities." But trust and obligation are an objectification of conducts and consist in non-personal performances. They may call for certain "character types" and not others, e.g., the international civil servant and not the crusader. Essentially, an ethic of rights suppresses personality and community. Thus, critics are correct in describing an ethic of rights as abstract and legalistic, but they are mistaken when they condemn it for that reason.

Indeed, I subvert the proper duties of agents if I try to take account of their humanity, i.e., treat with them as if our relationship were interpersonal. They are expected to act within roles and prescriptions and so am I. As we say, "justice is blind." Conflict of interest, prejudice, special pleading and the like are evidence of a failed objectivity. To be sure, agency is performed by persons not robots. So, agents are going to be subverted by personality. Agency, then, is a struggle between wholeness and function. As the recipient of an agent's acts, I too am bound by function, am party to that same struggle. An interest in biography—well intended and not on the face of it morally dubious—is also subversive. If I gossip with the bus driver about family and friends, either the bus will never move or if it moves it may well cause an accident. I have diverted the attention of the driver as driver. Similarly, friendliness and kindliness are not necessary criteria for licensing someone as a surgeon or an engineer. Nor are friendliness and kindliness legitimate grounds for deciding which patient to treat or which client to serve. By contrast, an ethic that permeates life-world spaces relies on empathetic relationships, relationships of culture and intimacy. So what is subversive in the global domain becomes boorish in the interpersonal domain.

An ethic of rights, suitably described, can apply across the species, to its relationships to the environment in which it finds itself including other species, and to the varied groupings into which members of the species are organized. An ethic of rights deals with rules and roles. Its terms are "fairness," "equity," "objectivity," "reasonableness," i.e., justice terms. Where the moral legitimacy of a rule is challenged, it is by a supervening rule. For example, "I was only following orders" is not a defense precisely because a more general rule is invoked as in the Uniform Code of Military Justice or in provisions for conscientious objection or in codification's of the rules of war. Of course, to submit rules to other and more comprehensive rules is also to confess that, except for the moment, there is no final stopping point. But that is to call attention to the fact that an ethic of rights is always incomplete, is always historical.

Of course, there are problems here too. If rights emerge over time, retroactive assessments are on shaky ground. It becomes necessary to show that a more comprehensive rule was already present to consciousness even if not explicitly articulated. Often, this can be done, but not always. For example, a review of the Nuremberg trials reveals a double approach. Comprehensive rules were in fact "discovered," e.g., in the rules of war, the Geneva conventions and the like. As courts ordinarily do, these were re-interpreted to account for new conditions leaving open the problem of "judge-made" law and "original intent." However, in a nod to post-war opinion, arguments were also invented behind a screen of universality and timelessness. Thus, the notion of "crimes against humanity."[13] These were defined by reference to "human rights" and its forerunners, "god-given rights," "natural rights" and "self-evident rights." This allowed for both precedent and the appearance of moral substance. But, in practice, the language of human rights was transformed into procedures and procedural judgments, i.e., informed consent, "lawful" orders, due process, and the like. Duties and, in particular, prohibitions followed.[14] Left obscure was the question of rightful authority, i.e., the ambivalent status of victor and judge.

Rules, however, rely on a special notion of authority that may offer a way out. Moral competence is a corollary of role-competence. Thus, to assume a role is to warrant the possession of certain abilities, to agree to certain relationships, and to deny certain others. I think, for example, of the notion of a "profession" and the emergence of a professional "code." Where profession is expanded—I'm not talking about a nominalism which calls every job a profession—moral competence is similarly expanded, a further recognition of the incompleteness of the moral world. Role and code embody promises that are morally intelligible within a framework of rules not of ends.[15] Such promises have a certain grammar, set criteria of performance, and do not rely on feelings, past history, associative relationships, and the like. Following Kant, they rely on the "good will" which reveals once again their objectivity, i.e., the "good will" is a rational construct and not a matter of psychology or taste. So, moral competence fits a species-world, allows us to transcend a life-world. For example, international courts like those at the Hague or those hearing cases in sub-Saharan Africa draw upon plural legal and moral traditions.

An ethic of rights, then, is not lifeless nor does it lack its metaphors. In that sense, to accuse it of legalism, where this is taken to mean a kind of mechanicalism, is to miss the liveliness of performance and promise as well as of frustration and dereliction, i.e., the interaction between rights and events. This interaction is more like the logic of a Bach fugue than a jazz improvisation but no less attractive for all that. The tension of performance within restraint is its aesthetic.

I know that moving away from personalist morality is frustrating, particularly in a neo-romantic era—an expressivist era—like our own. In a deep sense, ethics is intimate: my judgments and my responsibilities, my subjectivity. But, intimacy is taken to extremes when conscience becomes absolute. Self-righteousness, self-indulgence, and authoritarianism become moral habits. Without recognizing the kinship, moral nihilism—its all a matter of taste—is their liberal embodiment. I spell out what counts as *the* good life. Similarly, I spell out what counts as *the* wasted life, *the* foolish life, even *the* wicked life. I may not be aware of what I am doing, however, just because I enjoy widely shared moral agreement within my life-worlds. Traditionalist or liberal, I am fooled by their pervasive influence into believing that my sense of the moral life is everyone's or ought to be.

An ethic of rights recalls in another way the democratic expectation. To be sure, democracy can be elaborated as a "way of life" within a particular life-world. But a global ethic finds a different democracy. It is a way of organizing the shared-world, the species-world. By implication, then, it is possible to be democratic in the species-world and non-democratic in the life-world. For example, a military unit, an emergency medical team, or a team sport may be authoritarian without subverting a democratic species-world. A Roman Catholic may accept the absolute authority of the Pope in faith and morals and still be a democrat within the species-world. Nor does this justify accusations of hypocrisy. Bad faith only appears when those within a particular life-world claim authority over those who are not members of that life-world,[16] i.e., when being non-democratic turns into being anti-democratic. Thus, fundamentalism is a denial of the species-world, is a model of bad faith. As a global expectation, democracy commands us to limit ourselves, to respect boundaries.[17] Democracy then, has radical consequences for our moral habits and desires, i.e., the habit of life-world domination.

There is no proof for the moral validity of any claim of "right." "Self-evidence" and the rule of reason—the Enlightenment favorites—only name the fact that rights are axiomatic and in that sense logically arbitrary. More usefully, "rights" may be understood as workable moral hypotheses arising within history. Like all hypotheses, rights evolve and change. This is all to the good. Rights do not become rigid, non-responsive, and ultimately irrelevant. Of course, the "uncertainty" that this entails generates a problem of moral commitment. It is difficult to see why people would put their lives on the line in defense of an hypothesis. Not for nothing then has "rights talk" been embedded in mythic[18] notions like natural law or divine sanction. At the same time, human knowledge has grown more and more secure precisely as certainty—based in rationalism or revelation—has given way to uncertainty. It may well be, then, that grounding rights in experience will lead to a more usable ethic than we have enjoyed in the past.[19]

The customary language of inalienable rights masks the fact that rights have always evolved. Language is used to hide what is going on, much as Plato confessed the need to invent the "myth" of the gold, silver, and bronze souls in order to legitimate and interpret the social structure of the republic. The "royal lie" and the "legal fiction" in other words enable rights to command belief and loyalty but at the risk of exposure and consequent disillusionment. "Demythologizing" these, as is typical in our age, reveals the fact that rights have a history, but it also invites skepticism in face of false promises. Given the habits of the life-world, skepticism all too easily turns into cynicism.

But in the new global environment, cynicism is not warranted. Admitted or not, an ethic of rights emerges from the "funded experience" of the species and is verified by the fact that it evokes approval in practice. With experience, rights are amended to more nearly approximate an imagined ideal, e.g., some one or another of the Enlightenment's "natural" rights like life, liberty, equality, property, or the pursuit of happiness. But we forget that the ideal also evolves. Experience and ideal interpenetrate without any final end or terminal point for either. Of course, rights language pretends to ultimacy, so this movement is interpreted as refining, extending, or clarifying the meaning and range of fixed ideal terms.

The modern world was ushered in by the notion of "natural rights" and the twentieth century by the notion of "human rights." This move from "natural" to "human" reveals that rights develop as a function of changing perceptions, enriched capacities, and novel problems. As the means available for insuring rights become more accessible and more effective, the moral imagination expands their meaning. For example, communication technology makes it possible to identify violations of rights quickly and publicly. The ability to respond to violation also exists although we do not yet have the will to respond particularly where the great powers or clients of the great powers are involved. Similarly, the ability to conquer hunger and disease, i.e., to provide a necessary means for the right to life, have become far more adequate than they once were. Thus, as medicine becomes a scientific art, a right to treatment moves toward the status of "human" right. In general, then, we see a perfection of instruments giving birth to new or amended rights.

Rights also evolve as the moral territory expands, e.g., as the notion of what counts as a human being has been extended.[20] For example, in the brief period between 1948 and 1998, we have seen this happen to the *Universal Declaration of Rights*. Today, its language jars the reader by its use of the masculine form, i.e., "he, him, his;" and by a cosmopolitanism that ignores multiplicity. And finally, new rights may evolve as society evolves. For example, a "right to work" (Article 23 of the *Declaration*) and a "right to rest and leisure" (Article 24) may arguably be derived from the notions of a right to life and liberty under industrial conditions. These were simply not "live-options" under eighteenth century conditions.

I imagine that we have difficulty with the notion that rights like "life, liberty and security of person"[21] are in motion particularly when we realize that this may entail an elimination and not just an expansion of right. Yet, it would not do to forget that the "rights" of lords and barons insured by the *Magna Carta* have effectively vanished. "Property rights" have been radically circumscribed since Adam Smith and John Locke. Then too, rights have also been expanded as in a woman's right to her own body or the worker's right to his labor.

Even "self-evident" rights are in an important way "procedural." For example, no attempt is made to spell out the "good" life or the "happiness" to be pursued. The emphasis on procedure, in other words, opens the door to development and allows development to hide behind re-definition. The apparent moral substance—life, happiness—is a place-marker for thought at a given historic moment. Even the notion of "life" is not without its conceptual and practical difficulties. For example, the attempt to define death comes up against the stumbling block of defining life. We differ—as in the controversy over abortion—about when human life begins. We differ—as in the controversy over suicide—over how life is to be ended. We differ as to who "owns" life and whether or not life can be a "property" right as the language of ownership implies. As these differences are worked out in experience, the right to life changes even where the language is preserved.

To announce a right is simultaneously to announce a duty. But that is to announce another difficulty, particularly when we move from "negative" rights which command us to let things alone to "positive" rights which command us to do some thing. Of course, a right becomes empty without the means to exercise it. But with the command to do something, we also risk illegitimate crossings of boundaries, risk what is called "paternalism." The puzzle grows more complicated still because there is no *a priori* way to define what counts as a necessary means, what counts as an optional means, and what doesn't count at all. These things shift with culture, history, and knowledge. For example, as we become psychologically sophisticated we re-define necessity. We would be hard pressed then to establish a set of "basic needs" although we could more easily identify glaring absences, e.g., as in famine, drought, etc. We notice, too, that duty is not preference.[22] A "right" limits freedom whereas a preference—a value, a good—exhibits it.

Rights may be extended by agreement as in a "contract." But contract has both moral and legal meaning although we typically confound the two. I have rights as a citizen of the United States or as a member of a university faculty. I can see how these differ from those of citizens of other countries or from those of students. Certain rights then flow from the notion of memberships in particular life-worlds and are, as it were, local phenomena. Thus, the move from the "fact" of property ownership to the "right" of property ownership relies on a "social contract."[23] The move from a "right" *to* property ownership to "rights" *of* property ownership signals the further move from ethic to law, to legal contract. Species-rights can be expressed in contract language too. But here contract is a moral metaphor, an attempt to convey the notion of an exchange of obligations that do not have the force of law. But then we also have to distinguish species rights from local rights, i.e., how far the boundaries of the life-world are inviolable, how far the species-world may intrude. The on-going debate about these occurs within the framework of expectations—often mis-called necessities—and the consequent claims that attach to a person because he or she lives in both the species-world[24] and one or more life-worlds.

Rights cannot appear morally until they reach a level of consciousness. Once articulated, they may be extended by convention.[25] Thus, international law suggests a model as long as we do not forget that it need not be moral at all. It may only exhibit interests. An ethic of rights attaches to persons and life-worlds while international law typically attaches to sovereignties. Yet, it is possible to imagine moral conventions, moral treaties. For such conventions to be morally legitimate, the parties would have to be representative of the multiplicity of life-worlds. In such a process, agents of the sovereign, e.g., ambassadors, would be replaced by representatives of life-worlds.

A global ethic is distinct from international law. Thus, agents at UN and other multi-national bodies do not ordinarily represent life-worlds. The closest approximation of their memberships may be found in "non-governmental" representation—e.g., faith groups, communities of care—although the habit of nationality still dictates how that representation is organized. Indeed, life-worlds often cut across national boundaries as with the Kurds, the Serbs, etc. Nations thus speak to a different reality. A parliament of nations is not a parliament of peoples. In this regard, we would benefit from an exploration of the relationship between the Declaration of Independence and the provisions of the U.S. Constitution. Similarly, we can learn from the distinction between the *Universal Declaration of Human Rights* and the UN Charter. Of course, the moral and legal pathways may parallel each other, but they need not do so. The use of common terms should not obscure the fact of different intentions.

The test of whether or not a right exists is whether or not I am obligated not to violate it. Rights are "claims" of protection; some legal, some moral, some local, some international. For a global ethic, the task is to identify and establish claims which I am obligated, in so far as possible, to honor as a species member. That means that when I violate the boundary they protect, I am morally wrong.[26] But, am I duty bound to defend the rights of members of other life-worlds within their life-worlds? For example, must I defend the rights of women in the Roman Catholic Church or in Iran or Saudi Arabia?

Duties then are more limited than oughts. Duty, in other words, is not the whole of my moral life. So, I may argue, judge, seek to persuade, write editorials, and all the rest. But I am not derelict in my duty if I do none of these things. Although you may think me immoral, insensitive etc. if I remain silent, you cannot compel me to argue, judge, etc. This recognizes that my relationship to another's life-world obliges me *not* to act as if I had a species-world duty unless some kind of convention authorizes me to do so. More puzzling is the problem of the use of coercion—boycotts, blockades, threats—in order to enforce one interpretation of rights or in order to enforce one set of moral priorities over another.

An obligation to refrain is not equivalent to indifference. It announces the affirmative intention to be respectful of boundaries. It recognizes the fact that I am not obligated to members of other life-worlds in the same way that I am obligated to members of my own life-world. I am, however, obligated to all members of the species when species rights are invoked. For example, if a global ethic were to include a right to liberty, then it would authorize the invasion of all life-worlds where liberty was violated. If equality were to be a species right, then its violation would authorize yet another invasion. At the same time, diversity sets limits on how I am permitted to act in accordance with such duties, how I am to understand liberty and equality in a species-world. The work of a moral convention will be difficult since it authorizes me to cross boundaries.

A certain scrupulousness is a duty too. Inequality may be freely chosen, e.g., as in entering a community whose rules are announced in advance and as in having the freedom to leave such a community. My duty then is to insure that the rules are announced and that membership is voluntary. For example, that distinguishes the situation of women in Roman Catholicism from women in Iran or Saudi Arabia. Membership in a nation is unlikely to be chosen and freedom of movement is unlikely to be a practical option. Membership in a faith community, however, is more likely to be choosable although I do not underestimate the strength of tradition and family ties. I may also find myself with a duty to refrain and a duty to interfere. Rights may—probably will—conflict. I thus require a process of adjudication. A global ethic needs its moral institutions much as international law needs its juridical institutions.

Unfortunately, the use of rights language has become thoughtless not least of all because an effort has been made to talk of "positive" rights as in the *Universal Declaration*.[27] Despite obvious good will, such talk blurs an ethic of rights which can convincingly do its work only if kept limited, i.e., its transcending duty is respectful accommodation. It is not unusual, however, for anything that anyone finds morally desirable to be transformed into a rights claim. This is understandable given the popularity of rights talk and the obligatory nature of rights as against the voluntary nature of values. But as with any inflated currency, the consequence is that rights cease to have the force which they need. This tells us once again that there are many more "oughts" than "rights." I ought to have good taste, to love my neighbor as myself, etc. But I'm not clear how these can fit with an ethic of rights. I cannot be coerced into loving my neighbor.

It is annoying to be told that a global ethic is a matter of "shalt nots." Yet, this is not quite as bleak an outcome as it might appear to be. A global ethic includes the right to be let alone, the right to exercise freedom of choice, the right to live as one wishes, etc. The point of a global ethic is to insure that such rights are honored in at least two ways: by establishing a duty to protect against violations and by establishing the means for making such rights actual and not merely formal. But I do not wish to be misunderstood. I would not be ambitious about the means and would see them as limited as in a freedom to travel, a right of privacy and the like. In other words, means should not become the excuse for transforming negative into positive rights. Finally, another consideration leads me to insist on limitation. Since a duty follows on a right, coercion is morally legitimate. That would certainly call for moral caution. Duties are not voluntary and deliberate failure to do one's duty is rightly punishable.

Imagination and a Global Ethic

To sum up: the remarkable fact of our age is the democratic expectation. At the same time, the need for a global ethic emerges from the tension between the ethics appropriate to life-worlds and the ethics appropriate to the species-world.[28] A global ethic is the outcome of this dialectical geography. Because the moral life under conditions of democratic expectation calls for us to make room for the variousness of persons and communities, a global ethic must be minimal. Its task is to establish the least onerous conditions for respectful accommodation. But I am trained to identify life-world morality—as long as it is my own life-world—as common morality. That is neither possible nor desirable. That means, that a global ethic is going to be deeply unsatisfying to my moral habits.

In a similar way, the traditional grounding for "rights" has become problematic. It is not possible to discover a species-wide meaning for notions like "nature," "god," "human being," "moral" etc. To assert these and like notions as if they were genuinely universal is to engage in moral blindness or covert aggression. It is for this reason that I have suggested that rights are to be viewed as hypotheses, that the appropriate mood is uncertainty, that the appropriate process is evolutionary and that the appropriate metaphor is contractual.

So, a global ethic needs a moral education which teaches the uncertainties of ethics. New moral habits are needed as good and evil have grown more various and so more ambiguous. Even their identification is a puzzle. Indeed, it is often difficult to decide between them because of the doubts that inhere in the situation rather than because of the saintliness or villainy of the human beings involved. Further, a global ethic requires a scrupulous respect for the distinction between life-world and species-world. However, caution, restraint, limitation, and the making of distinctions is a tedious and unromantic business. We have been taught, instead, to enjoy the moral crusade and to celebrate moral simplicities. These lessons must now be unlearned.

A global ethic cannot have the richness and depth of a life-world ethic. It will, as it were, be aesthetically minimal too. Certainly, at the outset, it will lack the supports of biography, tradition, and culture. This tells us that communicating a global ethic in an attractive and convincing way will be difficult. Verifications beyond the bare bones of law and logic will be hard to come by and will need the time of history. A global ethic will not at first, fit with our moral intuitions and its ability to reconstruct moral intuitions will lack the resource of tradition. Language itself will be a problem since natural language arises within life-worlds, e.g., compare the strained and artificial languages of transnational activities, the confusions of translation. Then too, a global ethic comes into being as a criticism of its own history and as a departure from its own history, i.e., as a denial of conquest, of imperialism, of cosmopolitanism, of assimilationism. To that extent, it starts as a counter-history, is conveyed by negations. Ironically, that forecasts the possibility of a future richness. Opposition and resistance after all evoke heroism and motivate epic. But a counter-history has barely begun.

Telling the story of the species-world will need its own genre. Myth, drama, dance, and music have been the vehicles for rooting values and purposes. With them, we share our hopes and dreams, our fears and anxieties, our ideals and failures. The communal arts set values and purposes in place. But globe is not community, not a folk culture. So, a global ethic inverts the aesthetic process. It begins in self-consciousness. It is rightfully rationalist and critical. It lacks the mystery which is art's birth-mother. Its is even more problematic because it is not just self-conscious but a "second-best."[29] So when we try to speak globally, the words are denatured, legalistic, and prosaic. The symptom is the endless flow of paper at UN or the mathematical languages of the sciences.

And yet, there are hints. The globe will have its own sins and its own sinners just because the species-world is a scene of its own rights and duties. So, demanding that the species conform to a single comprehensive moral code would be a sin. Prescribing a single vision of the good life would be a sin. Allocating privilege and punishment in the species-world using the values of the life-world would be a sin. A global ethic then has its personal commandments too, above all "thou shalt not impose your morals on others unless they ask you to do so."

Nor is the tragic sense without its possibilities. A global ethic leaves in place much that is morally doubtful or even morally evil. It means that the horrifying and the villainous within life-worlds are beyond its reach in principle and not just in practice. So we live with the struggle that cannot be victorious. Tragedy as usual mixes with comedy, with satire. Our ethical pretensions are grander than our moral practices. Indeed, the gulf between language and practice is precisely why, I suspect, ethics is greeted with disbelief and even with cynicism. An ethic of uncertainty is more constructive. It elevates respect to a species-wide characteristic and multiplicity to the level of principle. In this way, it breaks the chains that have historically bound men and women to place and power. It is finally heroic.

A new global ethic puts in place an ultimate equality of members of the species—equality of choice, for example—and honors the choices they make. This, in turn, suggests the style of a new global ethic. Austere and negative as it may seem, a global ethic is built on appreciations. For much too long, the species has torn itself apart in the effort to impose one life-style, one life-world, one ethic on all of its members. To legitimize life-world and species-world dissipates the historic imposition. In its place is a globe with many ways of living and working and dreaming, and yes, suffering. Rather than complain of a varied humanity, a global ethic invites its celebration. Uncertainty thus turns into an affirmation. It is the chance to increase knowledge and to delight in its opportunity. Looking backward, a global ethic breaks into the past. Looking forward, it opens to richer worlds of experience.

Notes

1. See by way of example, Richard Rorty, *Contingency, Irony, and Solidarity* (New York: Cambridge University Press, 1989).

2. As the *New York Times* reported, "When Congo's president, Laurent Kabila, got ready for a trip to Europe last week, he sent an advance party to Belgium...to seek assurances that there would be no nasty surprises waiting—an arrest warrant for example...'Tremble tyrants!' was the editorial message the Paris newspaper *Liberation* sent to a list of dictators after a panel from Britain's House of Lords...ruled Wednesday that the former Chilean dictator...was not entitled to immunity from arrest under a British law protecting former heads of state." (November 29, 1998). While the matter is still *sub judice,* its occurrence is instructive.

3. While anecdotal, perhaps, the conference in Korea at which these ideas were first discussed was illustrative. It included representatives from most Asian nations as well as Westerners and some sub-Saharan Africans. The language of equality, freedom, and rights translated easily, did not fall on deaf ears and was, indeed, part of the common currency of the discussion.

4. Inquiry into the implications of the Enlightenment is to be found, in part, in my essay, "Reconstructing The Enlightenment—Toward A Sociable Democracy," Kyung Hee University, September 1994.

5. John Rawls speaks of "reflective equilibrium" which is another way of making the point. See *A Theory Of Justice* (Cambridge, Mass.: Harvard University Press, 1971), pp. 48-51.

6. This essay is not the place to develop a full notion of "life-world." For my purposes, it is sufficient to note that life-worlds include family and clan, religious, work, and avocational communities, etc. There is no *a priori* way of limiting the list. Within life-worlds, persons find themselves, find others with shared languages and values and purposes, etc. Within life-world persons develop. I use the term life-world rather than community because it conveys the psychological and biological characteristic of the experience. A life-world is not simply a cultural artifact.

7. I use the term "language" generically to stand for communicative structures—signs and symbols—that carry the practices and values of given life-worlds. Thus it includes "natural" languages like English or Chinese and non-traditional languages like those associated with the sciences, e.g., mathematics, technical skills, e.g. computer-speak, professional jargons, e.g. medicine, or life-style choices, e.g., teen-age speech.

8. There is an extensive philosophic and political tradition which speaks to the question of limitation in the name of freedom. In the west, the classic statement of this is, no doubt, John Stuart Mill's *On Liberty* (1859; reprint, London, England: Penguin Books, 1974).

9. I admit that I hesitate to use the word, "secularity" because we are likely to hear it as "secularism." But "secularism" is a type of ideology and advocacy as are other variations of humanism. Indeed, it is the failure to understand the distinction between species-world and

life-world that accounts for the failure of humanism to attract and sustain its own community. In any event, secularism is not a synonym for secularity and is quite a different matter from the material possibilities and expectations which transcend all life-worlds.

10. In the Western tradition, we may represent this distinction by referring to Immanuel Kant and Aristotle. The former identifies ethics with universal moral law, the latter with a plurality ends gathered under the word "happiness" and guided by the notion of the "golden mean," i.e., neither too much nor too little. A permeating ethics, would obviously not choose between these but see them as complementary features of moral experience. I suspect, but do not know, that the Buddhist tradition incorporates both as in the "middle way" and "nirvana." On the other hand the Confucian tradition seems much more Kantian than Aristotelian although its focus on right practices does have an Aristotelian ring to it. At any rate, I would guess that the Western distinction is replicated in a number of different ways throughout the world.

11. Feminist literature in the United States and elsewhere has been particularly critical of "rights" and "justice" approaches to ethics. Correctly, it is pointed out that the good life is embedded in relationships, in a "network" and that terms like concern, love, empathy, sentiment and care are ethically relevant although usually absent from most Western moral discourse. See, for example, Carol Gilligan, *In A Different Voice* (Cambridge, Mass.: Harvard University Press, 1982) and Nel Noddings, *Caring, A Feminine Approach to Ethics and Moral Education* (Berkeley, California: University of California Press, 1984).

12. See Howard B. Radest, *Community Service, Encounter With Strangers* (Westport, Conn.: Praeger, 1993).

13. For a discussion of Nuremberg trials and problems of legitimacy, of ex post facto law, of imposition of rules by victors over vanquished, etc. see two articles by Robert Baker, "A Theory of International Bioethics: Multi-culturalism, Post Modernism, and the Bankruptcy of Fundamentalism," and "A Theory of International Bioethics: The Negotiable and the Non-Negotiable," *Kennedy Institute of Ethics Journal* 8, no. 3, (September 1998): 201-231 and 233-273.

14. This negative formulation is derived from the Hebrew Bible. The Christian formulation is "Do unto others as you would have them do unto you" but that positive formulation permits me to impose my

values upon you even if beneficently and this is precisely what must be denied in a diverse world. Finally, the Kantian formulation, the "categorical imperative" might be taken as a usable guide: ask yourself whether you would wish the rule (maxim) you are now following to be a universal rule. No doubt every tradition has some formulation of this notion of moral reciprocity.

15. In this regard, it is interesting to look at medical codes. While there may be some reference to "health," the operative requirements and prohibitions specify behaviors to be undertaken or rejected. Further, while "health" makes for an interesting discussion—what is it, how do we know it—such discussions are usually indeterminate and so not very helpful in conduct whatever use they may have in clarifying ideas and exploring possibilities.

16. I understand that some claims from within some life-worlds are by nature intended to be global. But, unfortunately for such claims, the notions of democracy and diversity require that such claims be denied. Nothing, of course, prevents anyone or any group from arguing for the universality of its claims. And nothing, morally, prevents anyone from simply denying them or even refusing to listen.

17. Obviously, this point derives its historic meaning from the notion of sovereignty. But, for a global ethic, it might be interesting to use sovereignty metaphorically and not legally and thus to extend the notion to life-world and individuals.

18. I do not use the word "mythic" to mean falsity. A myth is an explanatory story, an interpretation of reality which provides meanings.

19. See John Dewey, *The Quest for Certainty* (1929; New York, Capricorn Books, 1960).

20. For example, the 1948 Declaration recognizes that persons cannot be property in Article 4: "No one shall be held in slavery or servitude; slavery and the slave trade shall be prohibited in all their forms."

21. This is the text of Article 3 of the *Universal Declaration of Human Rights*, 10 December 1948.

22. In this sense, Immanuel Kant correctly foresaw that an ethics of rights required doing duty "for duty's sake" and that this created a categorical and not just a conditional imperative.

23. From John Locke onward, the "social contract" has included the notion that property is a consequence of joining labor to natural resources. But the existence of a property "right" requires a political agency for its enforcement. At that point, by the way, the right of "private property" is a social invention and it could not exist without a political entity. To require the owners of property, then, to meet social obligations—taxation, etc.—is a legitimate recognition of the fact that the rights of ownership are served by society and could not be met without it.

24. There are, as we can easily see, different kinds of rights. The question for a global ethic is to find out what counts as "natural rights" or "moral rights" or "human rights." While these three terms are somewhat different—particularly in identifying the sources of rights—they point in the same direction, i.e., to what counts as species rights. For a discussion of these distinctions, see Joel Feinberg, *Social Philosophy* (Englewood Cliffs, New Jersey: Prentice Hall, 1973).

25. This was illustrated in a striking way in a recent address by Kofi Annan, the UN Secretary-General. He "challenged big business...to enter into an unusual and formal 'compact' with the United Nations to promote human rights, labor and environmental practices in the lands where they do business. In return, he offered UN political support for 'the open global market.'" Alan Cowell, "Annan Fears Backlash Over Global Crisis," *The New York Times* (February 1, 1999).

26. See Ronald Dworkin, *Taking Rights Seriously* (Cambridge, Mass.: Harvard University Press, 1977).

27. For example, Article 16 (3): "The family is the natural and fundamental group unit of society and is entitled to protection by society and the State." Or, Article 25 (1): Everyone has the right to a standard of living adequate for the health and well-being of himself and of his family, including food, clothing, housing and medical care and necessary social services, and the right to security in the event of unemployment, sickness, disability, widowhood, old age or other lack of livelihood in circumstances beyond his control." Obviously, there is nothing morally wrong with these provisions except that as "rights" they extend the territory of duty beyond what may be reasonably de-

manded of others. A right, after all, permits of little flexibility and presumes a minimum amount of conflict between rights and duties. Yet, in a famine situation or in other situations of drastically limited resources, I am not sure that my duty to honor your right can or ought to override my duty to my family, etc.

28. I am aware of recent debates on "animal rights" and "ecological ethics." Yet, I think we have enough to do for now to deal with our species. Down the road, our relationships with other species and with "nature" itself will require a further evolution of a "global ethic." But that is for another time and place.

29. In this connection, it is interesting and useful to compare Plato's *Republic* with his *Laws*. The former is grand drama; the latter is prosaic analysis and prescription.

11

THE POSTMODERN CHALLENGE TO A HUMANIST AESTHETIC

Carol Wintermute

In recent times there is a return to viewing art as providing truth about human experience and nature. Some theorists like Nelson Goodman see art as having symbols and a language of its own that functions cognitively but in a way quite unlike the propositional discourse of science and moral reasoning, There is a current European critique of science as the only road to understanding. The claim is that there are other forms of knowledge, like art, which reach deeper to understand the human experience. Unlike science, art can live with ambiguity, indeterminateness, and nuance. In such views as these, propositional discourse is a form of representation, which is limited. It cannot get behind the empirical curtain to see the raw stage of the human condition. Truth exists, not because it corresponds to, or represents something, but because it exposes experience. Art is a form that opens nature to a language and pattern of thought that is different but equal to the scientific worldview.

In a previous article,[1] I gave a brief overview of some of the aesthetic propositions of philosophers and thinkers who are a part of
the development of the naturalist and humanist perspective in the
western world. The ancient Greeks had great respect and reverence
for art but were caught in a bind by viewing it as something that either mirrored nature's beauty, gave pleasure, or referred to some
perfect world belonging to the gods. In Plato's scheme, its value lay
in its imitation of the world of the Ideal forms beyond our everyday encounters.

The Italian Renaissance recovered the classical Greek naturalistic and materialistic aesthetic concepts that had been derailed by
Christian theological concerns with decorating God's house or seeing art as a means to reflect God's grand design. However, Renaissance thinkers were stuck in the Neoplatonic concern with har-
monic structures, symmetry, order, and fixed rules for imitating the
perfect form of the Ideal world.

Immanuel Kant took up where predecessors like the Earl of
Shaftesbury left off with his view of art as anchored in nature. Nature is the source of beauty and art enlarges upon it. The beauty we
humans resonate to in nature is a source of spiritual qualities. With
Kant there is an underlying spiritual reality that art expresses. Aesthetics for him is in the domain of human experience. Art is beautiful when it strikes a universal chord in minds and hearts. The
imaginative genius is one who is rich with aesthetic ideas. Art sym-
bolizes these ideas in the forms that it takes. The ideas are of the
spiritual realm of the beautiful and good that is beyond representation. The aesthetic experience for Kant is an emotional reaction to
the unique expression of the genius that can tap into this spiritual
realm of ideal beauty and good and present something of its essence
to us.

The German Absolute Idealists find spirit as an absolute, which is manifest in self-consciousness experience. Art reveals this spiritual reality and thus is the crowning human achievement. While adding the cognitive aspect to the emotional expression of Kant, the Idealists, like Kant, are still stuck with a world beyond this one to which art must refer. They also have the problem of art competing with science as a form of knowledge.

John Dewey is the philosopher who brings resolution to these dilemmas in mid twemtieth-century America. His aesthetic is where humanists must return if we are to answer some of the very legitimate criticisms laid upon us by postmodernist thinkers as exemplified by the multiculturalists and neo-feminists. Their critique of humanism, however, points to thinkers prior to Dewey and they seem quite unaware of his correctives for the movement.

Art, for Dewey, is experience. It is a process. It is a social interaction. The artist is a person who employs imagination to link his/her personal experience to the vast stream of experience, which is common to human beings, by creating a work that is immediately recognized by the audience as an individual expression of that shared experience. The artist moves back and forth between the general experiences of humans to the particular one that s/he is illuminating. The artist also moves back and forth between what s/he is making and how the observer will perceive it. Observer and perceiver are inaccurate terms because the person on the receiving end of the artwork is always taken into account as part of the process. The receiver is part of the creation because s/he is part of the community of humans who have partaken of life's unfolding to which the artist is referring in his/her unique way. The receiver is also necessary to the art experience because it is s/he who determines if the artwork, indeed, struck some universal nerve, and spoke to a truth of experience in a language that amplified, highlighted, and emphasized that experience in a form that is exquisite, beautiful, and meaningful. The beauty found in art is not mere representation of nature or something pleasurable to the eye, but that which strikes deep into our emotions and intellect because it has taken fragments of our life's experience and unified them into a whole expression that can bring intense fulfillment to our sense of being.

What Dewey has done is to raise art to its deserved status as a major domain of knowledge and human achievement. At the same time art is not a challenge to science, reason, or philosophy. Science is verifiable knowledge that describes our world. Reason is the tool we use to make judgments and draw logical conclusions for acting in the world. Philosophy is a system of thought for deriving meaning in life. Art is an imaginative process with cognitive and emotive elements that results in giving us meaning in a non-verbal language form that tells us something of the nature of human experience.

Dewey's aesthetic is rooted in this world of everyday reality. Art is not a symbol for another realm of the Ideal or theological embodiment of the Good. It may, through the play of imagination, help to illuminate our actual world, clarify our hopes and give intimations about future possibilities resulting in the good, but art's job is the earth-bound one of exploring the mundane, average, normal things of living and finding the painful and pleasurable depths and heights within this material.

Dewey has eliminated the duality of this world and other, the duality between emotion and intellect, the separation of artist and audience, the separation of individual from community, and the competition of art with science, reason and philosophy for knowledge and understanding.

Now let's look at what the postmodernist thinkers are saying and if Dewey has any answers for their critique of the aesthetics of humanism.

Jean-Francois Lyotard, in *The Postmodern Condition: A Report on Knowledge,* says,

> Here, then, lies the difference: modern aesthetics is an aesthetic of the sublime, though a nostalgic one. It allows the unpresentable to be put forward only as the missing contents; but the form, because of its recognizable consistency, continues to offer to the reader or viewer matter for solace and pleasure. Yet these sentiments do not constitute the real sublime sentiment, which is an intrinsic combination of pleasure and pain: the pleasure that reason should exceed all presentation, the pain that imagination or sensibility should not be equal to the concept.
>
> The postmodern would be that which, in the modern, puts forward the unpresentable in presentation itself, that which denies itself the solace of good forms, the consensus of a taste which would make it possible to share collectively the nostalgia for the unattainable; that which searches for new presentations, not in order to enjoy them but in order to impart a stronger sense of the unpresentable.[2]

I think what Lyotard is saying here, is that modernism is a failed promise. Since its aesthetic is an attempt to represent the essence of reality in some totality, it is engaged in a futile enterprise. Since it's a representation, it is not the real thing. It can only provide its audience pleasure or pain in some form. But the essence of life is tied up somewhere between these two elements and no amount of reasoning or imagining can get at it. Thus, why not forget the attempt to get at some universal truth in art and go in the direction of presenting all the different elements, which are out there in specific and personal instances. There are no rules for creating or judging art in the postmodern view; the work itself is searching for them. It is not until it's finished that one can begin to understand what governed its creation and then it's too late because the event is over and each new artistic event will start afresh looking for its rules, which cannot be derived from any previous work.

This is but one example of the phenomenon of postmodern thinking. Whatever modernism proposes, which is the formations of western humanists, is to be countered by its opposite in the postmodern reaction. In architecture, for example, modernism expresses a renewed faith in the rational. It was stylistically to be the expression of organic unity of form and function in its simple essence. Postmodern architecture heads off in the opposite direction of bringing together incompatible elements that are in a constant process of collaborating. The individualism and unity inherent in modern architecture is challenged by postmodern architectures hybrid multivalent structures like Philip Johnson's A T & T Building in New York, which is a steel and glass tower capped by a Chippendale pediment that makes the whole thing look like a grandfather's clock. To the modernist eye, it is disjointed, incongruent, and a false illusion. To the postmodernist, it presents an ironic unity in the disparity between contemporary and antique, function and decoration, and domesticity and public life by exploiting these differences. The purpose, unlike modernism that attempts to present reality, of postmodern architecture is to invent allusions to the conceivable that cannot be presented.

In painting, modem art reaches it culmination in abstract expressionism. It had withdrawn from the task of representing the world and could now focus on the purity of its own art form. Painting's unique characteristic among art forms is its two-dimensionality. It is this aspect, which abstract painters explored to create a formal unified language of expression. The principle of unity was applied to the internal logic and coherence of the artist's use of materials on this two-dimensional plane. The social and political worlds are detached from painting so it can realize itself and its true nature.

Postmodern painting breaks down this norm of integrity by displaying a multiplicity of styles and methods that acknowledges its artificiality. It can encompass a mixing of incompatible styles, schools of painting from past history, images from other cultures all in a sense of ironic global village cosmopolitanism. Diversity is the key; nothing is to be excluded as in modernism. The result is that since there is a wide range of experiences contained within, there is no single interpretation that can account for this diversity. In postmodern painting representation, symbolism, and connotation are all present so that one cannot tell from this allegory what the main story is or to what it alludes.

Another aspect of postmodern painting is the doing away of the avant-garde. These elitist practitioners who concentrated on shocking the bourgeoisie and the art public have prevented art from being, what it always was in essence, thoroughly bourgeois. Therefore forms of art considered taboo by modernists are back in vogue. Bad art is in. The modernists banned it because while technically skillful, it expresses banal sentimentality.

A recent article in *The New York Times Magazine*, discusses this eventuality. On one hand, Deborah Solomon is pleased that the reign of abstraction is over. She says,

> For much of this century, the art that was hailed as quintessentially modern belonged to a single category—abstraction—and though Picasso never went completely abstract, his Cubism was viewed as the Big Band that made all forms of art life possible. Abstract art was not easy to understand, and it led the American public to think of museums as intimidating places ruled by a cadre of experts whose taste and rituals seemed as mysterious as those of Byzantine priests.[3]

She sees "bad art" as not only a backlash at modernism but also a yearning for the safe and reassuring past that the avant-garde renounced. Postmodern art historians are applauding the erasing of the line between paintings of Elvis on velvet, coke cans labels and Michelangelo's Sistine Chapel. Today the avant-garde abstractionist works, pop and op art, and protest works are so accepted, they are classics and what is truly outrageous is middle and low brow art. It is Norman Rockwell in his glorious current revival. David Hickey, a professor of art criticism and theory say that bad art is not just a clever postmodern stance. It is a genuine nostalgia and affection for the "whole messy pell-mell lot that is American culture."[4] As Solomon points out, it seems that in our postmodern world sentimentality is the symbol of our era.

Notes

1. *Humanism Today* 13 (1999).

2. Stephen David Ross, ed., *Art and Its Significance: An Anthology of Aesthetic Theory* (Albany: State University of New York Press, 1984), pp. 563-4.

3. Deborah Solomon, "In Praise of Bad Art", *New York Times Magazine* (January 24, 1999).

4. Ibid.

12

PRAGMATIC PLURALISM

Howard G. Callaway

This paper approaches "multiculturalism" obliquely via conceptions of social and political pluralism in the pragmatist tradition. As a matter of social analysis, the advent of multiculturalism implies some loss of confidence in our prior conceptions of accommodating ethnic, social, and religious diversity: the conversion of traditional American cultural diversity into a war of political interest groups. This, and the corresponding tendency toward cultural relativism and "anything goes," is fundamentally a product of over-centralization and cultural-political exhaustion in the wake of the long ordeal of the Cold War. An over-emphasis on the political, and national centralization, have pressured our cultural variety toward more political forms, and "multiculturalism" is both product and backlash.

Many issues connected with the general theme of multiculturalism parallel philosophical debates on objectivity and the diversity of cultural perspectives. Successful treatments of these themes, drawing on the pragmatist tradition, need to be developed and applied to contemporary problems. The approach here emphasizes a relative autonomy of religious, ethnic, and cultural-racial groups, the need to be wary of both exclusion and self-insulation, and the roles of individuals in mediating group differences.

Background of Cultural Pluralism

Cultural pluralism as an explicit social philosophy arose in the United States around the time of World War I, as part of the influence of William James. James was a steadfast opponent of every variety of philosophical rationalism and monism, particularly that conducted in the grand idealist style. He set out his own alternative in his late work, *A Pluralistic Universe* (1909).[1] This influence of James represented a break with some tendencies of Peirce's thought, though it also has roots in Peircean pragmatism. It was subsequently carried forward by James's student Horace Kallen, by Randolph Bourne, and Alain Locke, and expressed in writings of John Dewey.

Dewey remarked, as early as 1902, on James's role in giving currency to pluralism. "The term pluralism," Dewey wrote, "is very recent in English," and James "has probably done more than anyone else to give it currency," though he remarks that Howison also employed the word "to denote the substantially distinct existence of free ethical personalities."[2]

There is a limited kinship between James's pluralism and the personalism of George Holmes Howison (1834-1916). Howison, however, stressed the autonomy of the free moral person, in somewhat the style of Schelling, to the point of making each person uncreated and eternal. Howison was more the idealist and rationalist in contrast with James certainly, holding that the world is a "spiritual reality" developing teleologically with God as the goal of the process. This concept may reflect something of the earlier ideas of Leibniz, where only God sees to the coordination of the otherwise atomized individuals and interaction is a kind of well-founded illusion. But in James, there is no overall plan to the world, and relations and interaction are intrinsic to reality.

An influence of versions of philosophical personalism on James's pluralism is pretty certain, since James was deeply influenced by the French personalist philosopher Charles Renouvier (1815-1903), sharing with him an emphasis on personal freedom and the concept of a finite God. Like James, Renouvier was a vigorous opponent of Hegelian or Absolute idealism. The kinship of James to Renouvier is greater than that between James and Howison, since James and Renouvier escape the controlling idealist holism according to which only the totality (or its original elements) can act with any independence.

James wrote in his *Essays in Radical Empiricism* (1912) that his own philosophy "harmonizes best with a radical pluralism, with novelty and indeterminism, moralism and theism, and with the 'humanism' lately sprung upon us by the Oxford and the Chicago schools."[3] The last pair of references is to the work of the Oxford pragmatist F.C.S. Schiller and to John Dewey.

James argued, in a famous passage early on, that "The difference between monism and pluralism is perhaps the most pregnant of all the differences in philosophy:"

> Prima facie the world is a pluralism; as we find it, its unity seems to be that of any collection; and our higher thinking consists chiefly of an effort to redeem it from that first crude form. Postulating more unity than the first crude experiences yield, we also discover more. But absolute unity, in spite of brilliant dashes in its direction, still remains undiscovered, still remains a *Grenzbegriff.* "Ever not quite" must be the rationalistic philosopher's last confession concerning it. After all that reason can do has been done, there still remains the opacity of the finite facts as merely given, with most of their peculiarities mutually unmediated and unexplained.[4]

This Jamesian pluralism is a view about the general features of the world, both as we first encounter it and as it remains after the best efforts of reasoning have been applied. In spite of all our "brilliant dashes" in the direction of "absolute unity," the rationalistic philosopher is bound to admit that absolute unity is "ever not quite" within our reach, it remains a "limit concept." If James is right about this, then, the criticism applies not only to idealistic totalizing but equally to materialist or physicalist schemes of philosophical monism and reduction. The latter point emphasizes the relative autonomy of a plurality of distinct sciences and disciplines, and the differences in their typical objects or subject-matter, in opposition to the reduction of all to purely physical terms, whether motions of atoms in the void, or later versions.

James's pluralism was not merely an abstract philosophical doctrine. Social and political applications or lessons are frequently in the offing. Monism and absolutism are not merely philosophical errors, according to James, they are also and perhaps primarily social and political errors. For instance, there is a balance to be sought between the unity of the country and the diversity of its constituent social and political elements or units. This balance is reasonably sought in the intellectual and moral roots of American federalism and pluralism, as these have been contrasted with American nationalism. After the Cold War, we need to see again that liberal nationalism is always an unstable doctrine. America must be liberal and inclusive or it risks self-destruction.

James would surely agree with Theodore Roosevelt's warning that "the one absolutely certain way of bringing this nation to ruin, of preventing all possibility of its continuing to be a nation at all, would be to permit it to become a tangle of squabbling nationalities."[5] Notice how close this negative image comes to thinking of America's racial and ethnic diversity as formed into blindly contenting interest groups. But in some tension to this point, there is room to doubt that James would have greeted Israel Zangwill's concept of America as a "great melting-pot" with Roosevelt's enthusiasm for Zangwill's play.[6] The pluralistic thought is that we might all manage to be something of the "yankee-doodle dandy," while never quite melting together completely.

Sidney Ratner supplies the following short picture of Zangwill's play:

> But in 1908 Israel Zangwill, an English novelist and playwright who knew the United States well, wrote a play, The Melting Pot, which made the term and the idea part of American language and thought. In this play, the hero announces that America is God's Crucible, the Great Melting Pot where all the races of Europe are melting and reforming!...the real American has not yet arrived, he is only in the Crucible, I tell you—it will be the fusion of all races, the coming superman.[7]

What is objectionable here is not the idea that there is some melting of differences going on, or the idea that America is still in development. What is objectionable is a final fusion of all as an ideal. There is always more to our diversity and differences than can ever be *aufgehoben* into any higher unity we can, or will ever, foresee. "Ever not quite," as James put it.

Dewey was explicit on the point, famously holding that "the theory of the meltingpot [sic]" gave him "rather a pang."[8] This is partly because the idea of America as a great melting-pot, fails to distinguish between democratic interaction and mutual influence of diverse sources, on the one hand, and forced assimilation to a dominant paradigm, whether old or new, on the other. While emphasizing the value of democratic interaction among diverse cultural groups, Dewey wrote in the *Menorah Journal* that "the concept of uniformity and unanimity in culture is rather repellent:"

> One cannot contemplate in imagination that every people in the world should talk Volapuek or Esperanto, that the same thoughts should be cultivated, the same beliefs, the same historical traditions, and the same ideals and aspirations for the future. Variety is the spice of life, and the richness and the attractive-

ness of social institutions depend upon cultural diversity among separate units. In so far as people are all alike, there is no give and take among them. And it is better to give and take.[9]

The value of American diversity includes the diversity among American regions: "The United States is very much more interesting and more promising a place just because there is so much local diversity,"[10] says Dewey, and the point of insisting on their own differences and potential contributions was surely not lost on Dewey's intended audience. Given the value of diversity, it follows, too, that no matter how much our present differences may need to be reduced, on occasion, there should always remain room for them to grow or increase in other ways.

Similarly, to take a contemporary example, the rejection of cultural uniformity as an ideal is doubtlessly a crucial ingredient in the efforts at European unification. The Europeans simply do not want to be blended into some imagined uniform European culture. The idea is resisted on just about every side. But this does not mean that Europe sees no value in reducing those differences which have traditionally produced great tragic conflicts.

William James's similar comments are sometimes less clearly stated, in amongst his arguments against metaphysical or philosophical unifiers of various sorts. But it is surely part of his point in making such arguments that we may be held in the sway of a rationalistic, unifying image of the world to such an extent that we naturally carry it over into social and political thinking, even without being fully aware of doing so.

Pluralism and Open Community

James argues that "Pragmatically interpreted, pluralism" or the doctrine that the universe is many "means only that the sundry parts of reality may be externally related."

> Everything you can think of, however vast or inclusive, has on the pluralistic view a genuine "external" environment of some sort or amount. Things are 'with' one another in many ways, but nothing includes everything, or dominates over everything.

Looking at our social and cultural world pluralistically, each particular person or group must be seen to have its own partial autonomy and "external environment." Though no man or cultural group in America or elsewhere is completely an island, still, the degree or importance of relations to others is not everywhere or always the same. James continues:

> The word "and" trails along after every sentence. Something always escapes. 'Ever not quite' has to be said of the best attempts made anywhere in the universe at attaining all inclusiveness. The pluralistic world is thus more like a federal republic than like an empire or a kingdom. However much may be collected, however much may report itself as present at any effective center of consciousness or action, something else is selfgoverned and absent and unreduced to unity.[11]

So, James gives us very general grounds for thinking that we ought to recognize a degree of autonomy, and a right to self-definition, of any given social group as distinct from all the rest. As regards our ethnic, cultural, and racial diversity and differences, it is surely to the point to say that America, by tradition, has no national ethnic identity.

Most places are otherwise. There are nations for the Germans, for the Italians, for the Thais, for the Chinese, and many others. But America has always lacked an official ethnic definition suited to the relatively homogeneous standards of ethnically defined nationality.

We don't mind our hyphenated status as African Americans, Polish Americans, Mexican Americans, or Chinese Americans, say, so long as the "hyphens bind and do not separate" us to the point of Roosevelt's "tangle of squabbling nationalities." Other nations resist this kind of thing. We do not hear much about "Turkish Germans," or "African Frenchmen."

The basic definition of citizenship in Germany is ethnic, where in France, in contrast, it is defined by reference to a relatively thick common culture. American national culture is relatively thin in comparison, something more like a loyalty to on-going debates on our guiding political ideals. We traditionally have no recognized national religion, or costume, no single set of customs, no official language, color, or ideal of beauty. This is surely part of the reason that we have largely avoided the periodic life and death communal strife and national and tribal battles of others, enacted on their home grounds. It is also part of the reason why, except under duress, we never quite manage the same levels of national unity or centralization.

America's decentralized constitutional system creates greater unity and "great Presidents" only under conditions of stress; and otherwise, political power tends to flow away from the center. This is part of what makes our non-ethnic national identity possible. After fifty years of Cold War, we must learn again the need of this. Otherwise, the current degree of centralization will surely tend to support all manner of purely particularistic protest, political ideologies, and the yearning for excessive unity.

Viewed in a somewhat different perspective, America's ethnic and racial diversity is in significant degree a matter of religion. Often enough, that is, any given ethnic group can be seen to have a traditional religious definition or definitions. So, the Irish Americans are not simply Irish, but largely Irish Catholic, just as the Polish Americans are easily thought of as

Polish Catholics. Again the Scots-Irish, as we call them, are usually Presbyterian or sometimes they belong to similar Calvinist derived denominations such as the Southern Baptists. The Germans are largely either Catholic or Lutheran by tradition, the Scandinavians mostly Lutheran, and further examples are easy to produce. Along with the role of religion in defining the American communities of Italian, Polish, Irish, or New England British descent, it is difficult to think of an American ethnic or racial group more fundamentally active in religion than the African Americans. Recall that the civil rights movement largely arose from King's Southern Christian Leadership Council.

All in all, the *Harvard Encyclopedia of American Ethnic Groups* (1980) distinguishes over 100 ethnic groups in the U.S. population.[12] Highlighting the role of religious freedom and the separation of church and state in the development of American society, we might even say that our ethnic diversity has traditionally been socially organized by religious affiliations. In contrast to this, one important element of multiculturalism is the politicizing of ethnic difference as a matter of social-political loyalties and sometimes an Hegelian struggle for recognition. Removing the ideal aims of religious affiliations, I suspect, the result is likely to more resemble conflicting political interest groups.

I share the prevalent perspective among the pragmatists that the greatest weakness of American society is our tendency to dissolve ourselves into unattached or atomized individuals. This weakness is connected with our strength or virtue in avoiding the extremes of ethnic and racial conflicts, though of course, we don't always manage this either. But both of these characteristics of American society are strongly related to the relatively "thin" civic culture of the country. So, again, part of the point is that we have no "thick" national or common ethnic identity.

It is precisely these points which lead the pragmatists to their stress on community. Its social sources are akin to those of the strong tradition of American voluntary organizations. But in rightly emphasizing the need for community and the need to build communities, it is important not to mistake our own particular communities of memory, tradition, and affinity for a uniform overall American ideal.

Dewey wrote, most convincingly on the point in a frequently quoted passage from an article devoted to American nationality:

> No matter how loudly any one proclaims his Americanism, if he assumes that any one racial strain, any one component culture, no matter how early settled it was in our territory, or how effective it has proved in its own land, is to furnish a pattern to which all other strains and cultures are to conform, he is a traitor to an American nationalism. Our unity cannot be a homogeneous thing like that of the separate states of Europe from which our population is drawn; it must be a unity created by drawing out and composing into a harmonious whole the best, the most characteristic which each contributing race and people has to offer.[13]

"Our national motto, 'One from Many,' cuts deep and extends far," Dewey wrote, on the same page in 1916. Even external threat and war should not distract us from the point. What unity we can have must be created or composed largely by a democratic process of drawing out the best from all those who stand to make a contribution. This makes the task of building or maintaining national unity more complex, but it also holds out the promise that the result may be something greater than any of the parts could accomplish on their own.

Our national commitments, therefore, cannot be made at the expense of all other commitments. Though we may wish to bring out the best from those 100-plus American ethnic traditions, we are each in degree also tied to one or another of them, maybe even stuck there. This is the difficult idea which pragmatic pluralism needs to communicate. How do

we combine our own particularities with tolerance, acceptance, even encouragement to the contributions of others?
The answers are chiefly to be found in the openness of our
particular communities.

So, we ask what can be expected from our communities,
given that they are not to aim at becoming obligatory para-
digms for everyone. Lacking a national ethnic identity we
cannot afford to sacrifice all difference for unity. Instead we
have to find ways to build unity out of our differences, as
needed, and this point implies respect for differences of others as consistent with self-respect within our various particular communities of history, memory, and affinity. The last
thing we need is new emphasis on mutual exclusion in our
conceptions of community. That would be a communitarian-
ism with a vengeance. So, our particular communities must
remain open to outside influence and we require a certain
freedom to refuses rigid separation, segregation, or self-
insulation. In order that our particular communities can fully
or better understand each other, we require a certain openness of their boundaries, and some limits on competitions.

Continuity and the Logic of Pluralism

Synechism, the Peircean theory, insists that "continuity" is
"of prime importance in philosophy."[14] Whatever is intelligible, can be understood in terms of unbroken relations with
no absolute breaks or gaps. Rejecting the Kantian "thing-in-
itself" out of all relation to experience, and insisting on the
reality of relations, Charles Sanders Peirce shares themes with
the idealists and may seem to invoke an unrestricted holism.
But the theme of continuity does not exhaust Peirce's metaphysics, and it is worth noticing that James also uses the term
"synechism."

Differences arise in part from James's emphasis on a range
of relatively "internal" versus "external" relations, a theme

not emphasized by Peirce. If all relations obtaining between one thing and another were purely "internal," as for the Absolute idealists, then it would make sense to insist that all separation is falsification and that only the totality is genuinely and fully real, only the totality of truth is genuinely true. Common sense resists similar conclusions. My relation to my family, nation, or religion may contribute to my self-definition and identity, but it makes little difference to me, say, whether I live on a North-South street versus an East-West street.

My objective is not to explore or criticize the holistic and idealist notion, instead I want to briefly explore the resources available in Peirce suited to resist similar ideas. The Peircean concept of continuity is intimately related to his development and application of the logic of relations.

Now Peirce can be found to say that "The principle of continuity is the idea of fallibilism objectified."[15] This injects discontinuity and difference into the heart of the notion. "The doctrine of continuity rests upon observed fact," Peirce claims, "But what opens our eyes to the significance of that fact is fallibilism."[16] Once we become "fully impressed with the fact that absolute exactitude never can be known," we "naturally ask whether there are any facts to show that hard discrete exactitude really exists. That suggestion lifts the edge of that curtain," says Peirce, and we "begin to see the clear daylight shining in from behind it."[17] Fallibilism is a chief clue to Peirce's metaphysics. All measurement and observation involves inexactness and a margin of error, and is thus subject to error; but if all our evidence is inexact, we cannot conclude to an exactly definite and absolutely continuous reality on the basis of it.

"But fallibilism cannot be appreciated in anything like its true significance," Peirce proceeds, "until evolution has been considered."[18] Neither can "fallibilism objectified," i.e., Peircean continuity, be understood except in connection with

Peirce on evolution, which will bring us to the pragmatists's conception of development. Though spontaneity presents no instance of presently known uniformities or regularities, the unexpected is something to be expected in the world which Peirce envisages, and in view of the fact of evolutionary change, it is something which may lead on to new regularities. The emergence of new biological species, reproducing after their kind, is the most obvious case in point. This exemplifies discontinuity with structures heretofore developed.

If Peircean continuity is "fallibilism objectified," then this suggests that general continuity allows of local discontinuities. Continuity implies the regularity of systems of relations, but we do not suppose on that ground that every system of relations is absolutely continuous or allows of no breaks against a background of other relations. Thinking of continuity as fallibilism objectified, we will naturally expect that this allows for inexactness and even relative disruptions of systems of relations. The connection Peirce makes between continuity and evolution suggests the same point. For in evolution, against the background of species regularly reproducing after their own kind, we expect disruptions of regularity in the form of mutations which sometimes lead on to the development of new species and thus new regularities.

Another way of looking at related points is in terms of Peirce's criticisms of necessitarianism. In writings of 1903, Peirce distinguishes versions of the uniformity of nature, and takes a stand with one of these. The objective is to defend an Aristotelian conception of chance, as accident or coincidence. Peirce maintains that Boëthius misunderstood Aristotle's view of chance, and takes an argument from the *Consolations* to illustrate the mistake involved where the necessitarian argues against the Aristotelian conception of chance, as accident or coincidence.

> By a geographical fiction Boëthius represents that the Tigris and the Euphrates flow from a common lake. Now suppose a boat to be wrecked in that lake and one part of it is carried down the Tigris, the other part down the Euphrates, and where

these rivers, after being separate for hundreds of miles, flow together again those two parts of the boats are dashed against one another. There is a fortuitous event if there ever was one; and yet, says Boëthius, the currents forced them to move just as they did so that there was no chance about it.

So, was this a chance event or was it caused? No doubt, the flow of the two rivers respectively caused the two parts of the boat to arrive where they did at just the time that they did, but Peirce's point is not that chance in this sense involves any violation of natural laws, instead his point is that the coincidence in the working of the laws of nature is not itself always governed by law. Peirce continues:

> The event, it is true, was governed by the law of the current. But the fact which we are considering is that the two pieces that were dashed together had long before belonged together. That is a fact that would not happen once in ten thousand times, although when you join to this fact various circumstances of the actual event, and so contemplate quite another fact, it would happen every time, no doubt.[19]

What was accidental was that the two parts of the boat, which had once been joined, meet again as the two rivers meet, and this is surprising, something which we would not expect to be repeated. But it is part of Peirce's larger point that once we understand the laws and initial conditions involved in an accidental event, then we have the option to intervene in nature, controlling the initial conditions so that what was first purely accidental may become the first instance of a new regularity. In general terms, this is a way that Peirce has to provide for the evolution of law and the development of regularity. It is important to notice his very broad conception of the regularities of nature and its Aristotelian character. Regularity is what happens "always or for the most part."

The connection of all this to pluralism, concerns first the plurality of regularities, and their change over time—the development of new regularities, which may even serve to define a new domain of inquiry. Secondly we want to see some application of the basic ideas from Peirce to social development.

So, in place of the two parts of the boat and the two rivers, imagine distinct social groups. These may have some common origin in the distant past, but they have developed separately, in accordance each with its internal needs and the environments encountered. Now consider what can happen when these two social groups encounter each other. Immediately their environments are changed by the encounter. Such an encounter was not a regular feature in the continuing lives of the two groups, and often has an accidental character to it, involving the lack of mutual comprehension. But if we imagine that each has something positive to offer to the other, then something new and valuable has arisen through the accidental encounter, and once the sources of this are better understood, the two groups may proceed to reproduce the positive aspect of their interaction and control the negative aspects.

Similar ideas underline the pragmatist emphasis on communication and interaction. Although the emerging novelties of interaction are not always positive, and correspondingly, most biological mutations are in fact lethal, still social intelligence allows us to select and cultivate what is preferred and this may develop into new beneficial regularities. In general the social pragmatist see a pluralistic society as open to this kind of positive social evolution and development and as involving a richness which social monocultures lack.

Kallen, Locke, and Cultural Pluralism

Horace Kallen's conception of "cultural pluralism" has been dated to magazine articles from as early as 1915 and attributed to even earlier lectures.[20] Since Kallen was a student of William James at Harvard, there is every reason to relate Kallen's cultural pluralism to James's more general philosophical notion. Still the term "cultural pluralism" apparently only came into use following publication of Kallen's 1924 book *Culture and Democracy in the United States*.[21] While Zangwill's 1908 play might be seen as celebrating the immigrant's new-found freedom to escape the bounds of tradition and to freely interact, Kallen, in contrast, formulated a protest against xenophobia during World War I and the 1920s and against conformist versions of the melting-pot idea.

A Jew born in Germany, Kallen insisted on the right of immigrant groups to maintain their own integrity and autonomy, so that his original position has been described as "at the proto-separatist extreme of cultural pluralism."[22] His vision was of the United States as a "federation" of ethno-racial groups each maintaining its own distinctiveness. This was to be like a "symphony orchestra" in which each group would play together harmoniously with the others. His vision appealed to a number of American intellectuals, including the critic Randolph Bourne, who acknowledged Kallen as the inspiration of his famous article "Transnational America" (1916). Bourne definitely saw America's Anglophile tradition as the source of both American entry into World War I on the British side (which he resisted) and as the source of the demand for one-sided assimilation, in contrast to the influence of William James.[23] Still, it is worth mentioning that Americans of English and British descend have been among the most anglophobic among us, from the eighteenth century Adams's and Witherspoon to the twentieth century Lodges.

Kallen's contributions to a pluralistic philosophy of culture extended over a lifetime of writings. He persisted in using the melting-pot idea as a symbol of the rejected concept of forced assimilation, though there is certainly also recognition of the value of inter-cultural relations in his writings. This theme connects with his concept of the roles of individuals within and between groups. The thin common culture of the United States, which allows us to resist forced assimilation, is essentially a matter of the intercultural. In the 1956 book *Cultural Pluralism and the American Idea*,

Kallen speaks of the intercultural, the interfaith, and the interracial character of American culture:

> All three denote conscious ends and conscious means to attain the ends. All three are descriptive of the goals and methods in a teamplay of churches and of governments, urban, state and federal, as well as of voluntary ad hoc societies. The intent is in the common prefix: inter, which here postulates the parity of the different and their free and friendly communication with one another as both cooperators and competitors; it postulates that every individual, every society thus realizes its own being more freely and abundantly than it can by segregation and isolation and struggle to go it alone.[24]

Basically, I think there is no other way for America to be one country, consistent with the rejection of cultural uniformity as an ideal. It is not, certainly, that we expect all intercultural relations to be smooth and trouble free. But, by means of communication and interaction of groups and individuals, carrying or representing the various cultures, we do expect that democratic experience can grown and become fuller and more secure. Kallen's later views agree with the Dewey of 1939, in "I Believe," who said:

> I should now wish to emphasize more than I formerly did that individuals are the final decisive factors of the nature and movement of associated life...only the voluntary initiative and voluntary cooperation of individuals can produce social institutions that will protect the liberties necessary for achieving genuine individuality.[25]

Kallen commented in 1956 that this emphasis in Dewey's work might be looked on as an influence of his own earlier article "Individualism," and we can be certain that Dewey was then under the influence of the anti-Stalinist "Committee for Cultural Freedom," founded by Sidney Hook, among others, to help meet the twin threat of Stalinism and fascism. This liberal "Individualism" of Kallen's, like the related views of Dewey, recognizes the need of individuals for community, but refuses submission to collective egoism as the price.

While the term "cultural pluralism" originated with Kallen in resistance to forced assimilation, it was also employed in the pragmatist tradition, in protest against forced segregation. Here I want to mention some recent work due to Leonard Harris, Nancy Fraser, and Charlene Seigfried on the African-American philosopher Alain Locke (1886-1954). Locke is best known for his role as "midwife" to the Harlem Renaissance, and as an advocate of distinctively African-American art. But his cultural thought has recently gained recognition as a contribution to the pragmatist tradition.

Locke took an undergraduate degree at Harvard, studied at Oxford and Berlin and returned to take his Ph.D. at Harvard in 1918, where he worked first with Royce and finished with Ralph Barton Perry after Royce's death in 1916. Early on, and for a long time afterward, he was an associate of Horace Kallen. For nearly forty years, apparently including some disruption, Locke taught at Howard University, retiring as chair of the department in 1954. Based on his studies of African culture and its influences on Western civilization, he urged black artists to draw on African sources and to discover there materials and techniques for their work. He encouraged black authors to find subjects in black life and to set high artistic standards.[26]

Locke emphasizes race and race-consciousness, in common with many or most African-American intellectuals, and his conception of race is largely cultural rather than biological. Race, as he saw it is "primarily a matter of social heredity;" and thus "a fact in the social or ethnic sense," but it is an error to equate the fact of racial differences with a biological determination of culture.[27] According to Locke, his view leads "if soundly developed, not to cultural separation but to cultural pluralism." To be "Negro," he held, "in the cultural sense, then, is not to be radically different, but only to be distinctively composite and idiomatic, though basically American, as is to be expected."[28]

Locke makes room for African-American "racial," social, and political solidarity, while at the same time resisting racial or biological determinism. The concept is akin to the best in some nineteenth century conceptions, where "race" is not strictly distinguished from ethnicity and social culture. One key in Locke is that racial differentiation itself is subject to cultural conditions, and it may in turn influence cultural conditions.

Fraser provides the following characterization of the import of Locke's distinction between "civilization type" and "social culture:"

> More restricted than a "civilization type," a "social culture" in Locke's usage comprehends a substantive nexus of concrete life forms, including ethical horizons and interpretive traditions. Civilization type, in contrast, comprehends the more abstract, formal structures that subtend such life forms in a modern pluralistic society. Thus a single modern civilization type can encompass a plurality of social cultures. To invoke a language not available to Locke, members of different ethnicities, subcultures, "communities of value," and religious confessions, can all participate in the same civilization type.[29]

Assimilation to our "civilization type" is needed for full participation in American life, though this is not to be defined, and certainly not set in stone, by reference to any particular contributing social culture. So, while Locke provides resources for resisting forced assimilation to any established model of social culture, he also leaves the door open to democratic exchanges and mutual influences. Locke reclaims the American "melting-pot" from the specter of forced assimilation. As Fraser puts the matter, "Locke appreciates the emancipatory dimension of this ideal."[30] In some degree, if the ideas of assimilation and forced assimilation are kept distinct, then we all ought to be able to appreciate the same emancipatory potential. Even those Americans with British or English roots, after all, are not therefore British or English.

Locke's conception of a "civilization type," insofar as it can remain under debate and review, in light of the perspectives of various component social cultures, has some resemblance to the idea of a "thin" American national culture which allows for many variations on the unifying themes. This would appear to allow, too, for the conception of American national identity as a continuing arena of debate on unifying political ideals and mutual influences. Locke's writings may well repay further study.

Charlene Haddock Seigfried points to Locke's contributions to pragmatism, in her 1996 book *Pragmatism and Feminism*. In her chapter on "What is wrong with Instrumental Reasoning?" she says that in his 1942 book "Alain Locke sounded the alarm on the mainstream, positivist science that had continued to dominate in universities and institutions around the world, despite pragmatists's objections." Locke wrote:

> [W]ith the broadening scientific perspective on human social history that has been achieved one might logically expect enlightened social understanding and intercultural appreciation and tolerance. But this has not been so....people still read and write history from the chronic attitudes of cultural pride and prejudice, and sometimes deliberately, sometimes subconsciously, impose interpretations upon civilization that are steeped in cultural bias and partiality.[31]

The problem is that too much of theory about civilization and culture is a matter of "rationalizations" for claims and counter claims of ethnic, national, or racial groups, a matter of partisanship. In consequence, argue Seigfried and Locke, special interests and prejudices get reinforced with "the outward stamp of scientific objectivity and impartiality...and irrationality in social thinking grows apace."[32]

Elaborate systems of rationalizations may strengthen particular groups in conflict with others, as in the nationalist ideologies of old Europe. The danger is that the groups may become unable to communicate or solve outstanding problems. "According to Locke," says Seigfried, "racialist doctrines incite group rivalry as a weapon 'in the struggle for

group power and dominance, and it is of the greatest importance to see and understand them in this light. Carefully
analyzed, their major objectives are seen to be the justification of conflict and exploitation through the disparagement
of other group cultures and the promotion of prestige and
group morale through self-glorification and claims of superiority.'"[33]

The alternative to this kind of rationalization is an inter-
pretive social science and discursive forms of appreciation
which seek to bring out the best in the cultures of our concern. As Seigfried wrote in an another context, "James's
principled pluralism continually urges on us the importance
of sympathetically and imaginatively recognizing the specific
power of those who satisfactorily order their world differently from us."[34]

Pluralism versus Relativism

I quote below some passages from Sidney Hook's *The Quest
for Being* (1961) which speak directly to the issue of cultural
relativism. Hook puts his finger on a genuine problem of the
pragmatist tradition:

> The most common objection to naturalistic humanism is not
> that it has no place for moral experience but that it has no place
> for an authoritative moral experience except one that rests
> merely on arbitrary preference, habit or force. In consequence,
> it is accused of lapsing into the morass of relativism despite its
> desire to discover inclusive and enduring ends which will enable
> human beings to live harmoniously together.[35]

The intention is to base authority in the results of inquiry.
But if we think of inquiry as essentially open-ended (as of
course we do), then how can we call a stop to it to draw
conclusions? How do we know when we have had enough
inquiry? This must be a collective decision. But when we
come making a collective decision, how are we to prevent
the working of collective egoism of the kind which Locke

highlighted, irrational bandwagon effects, and so on? This is both a theoretical problem related to the tendency toward a purely process reading of inquiry (a metaphysics that over-emphasizes the continuity of inquiry (as against the discreetness of conclusions or results) and also a very practical problem in that the pragmatist tradition has been seen as sponsoring relativism; tendencies toward relativism have developed out of it, or under its influence.

As Hook continues, he stresses two elements of the problem. First that the emphasis upon solving specific problems in specific situations reinforces the impression of relativism, and secondly there is a prevalent confusion regarding the difference between claiming validity of results "relative" to situations and claiming validity of results in relation to situations.

> The impression that relativism is entailed by every form of naturalism is reinforced by the refusal of current humanists to content themselves with the affirmation of general ends certified to immediate intuition and by their insistence that ends must be related to means and both to determinate conditions of trouble and difficulty in specific historical situations. This makes value judgments in the only form in which they count, "relative" but "relative" not in the sense of subjective but rather relational.

Thus, Hook distinguishes relativity, which invites the charge of subjectivism, from relationality, which plausibly does not. If we are to use the term "relative" at all, then it does not contrast with "objective," instead it contrast with what is supposed to depend on no relations. Hook continues:

> The opposite of "relative" is not "objective" but "absolute" or "unconditional." This emphasis upon relational character reflects the dependence of value qualities, like all other qualities in nature, upon activities in process of objective interaction with each other. It should then be clear that the assertion "a value is related to a situation of concrete historical interests" and the further assertion that "a judgment of value is warranted when reflection indicates that what is declared valuable promises to satisfy these interests" does not add up to the view that anyone can legitimately believe that anything is valuable in any situation. On the contrary, inquiry into the relational character of

values, their historical, cultural and psychological reference, aims to find reliable values to guide action, reliable because they have objective grounds.[36]

So, Hook insists on the (potential) objectivity of results, even when such results (e.g., value judgments) relate only to specific situations and solutions to specific problems.

The obvious question, once we put aside the confusions of "relative" validity versus validity in relation to situations, is whether results which have been certified for given situations cannot be made to generalize over ranges of other situations. It seems clear that no one will object to the generalizations of chemistry, say, on the grounds that they have no application at the time, just after the "big bang" when the chemical elements had yet to form. So, results can retain application to a "limited" range of situations while still having what we would call a universal character: this is the idea of a domain of discourse, implicitly defined with reference to results obtained (and not "a priori").

What interests Hook is situations of conflicting values, and he observes that "One can hold to the belief in the objectivity of values without guaranteeing that agreement among conflicting values, all of which are objective from their own point of view, can be won."[37] The method which Hook shares with Dewey holds out the possibility of reaching agreement through further inquiry, but it does not maintain that such an agreement can always be reached (or, of course, that it can always be reached within time limits set by our prior expectations).

Hook's idea is that in situations of conflict, we may have to construct new values and interests "which will transform the conflicting values into a satisfying integrated whole."[38] (Very Deweyan, of course.) I suspect we must agree, in some sense, that "How far such an agreement can be won cannot be foretold until actual investigation into the conditions and consequences of value claims in definite situations is undertaken...."[39] Moreover, he insists that the idea that "an objective moral resolution of value conflicts is possible, entails the belief that men are sufficiently alike to work out ways of becoming more alike, or sufficiently alike to agree about the permissible limits of being different."[40] Interestingly, he also maintains that "The willingness to sit down in the face of differences and reason together is the only categorical imperative a naturalistic humanism recognizes."[41]

The point is of special interest, because it generalizes a value over all situations of conflicting values. This much generalization is implicit in the methodology which Dewey and Hook share. But it is of some importance to emphasize that not all differences, and not even all conflicts, immediately call for mediation. Or, to put the point in other words, one rational response to conflicts is entering into what James called the "and relation," and simply allowing different people to be different. We don't need to settle all of our differences in order to live in one pluralistic society. Sometimes, good fences make good neighbors, though we need to be wary of transforming fences into permanent barriers.

Notes

1. William James, *A Pluralistic Universe* (New York: Longmans, Green, 1909).

2. John Dewey, "Contributions to Baldwin's Dictionary of Philosophy and Psychology," vol. 2 (New York: Macmillan Co., 1902). Reprinted in John Dewey, *The Middle Works*, ed. Jo Ann Boydston, 15 vols. (Carbondale: Southern Illinois University Press, 1976-1983), 2:141-269, see p. 204.

3. William James, *Essays in Radical Empiricism* (New York: Longmans, Green, 1912), p. 90.

4. William James, *The Will to Believe and Other Essays in Popular Philosophy* (New York: Longmans, Green, 1897), p. viii.

5. See, Arthur Schlesinger, Jr., *The 'Disuniting of America: Reflections on a Multicultural Society* (New York and London: W.W. Norton, 1991), p. 118.

6. Ibid., pp. 32-33.

7. Sidney Ratner, "Horace M. Kallen and Cultural Pluralism," in *The Legacy of Horace M. Kallen,* ed. Milton R. Konvitz (London and Toronto: Associated University Presses, 1987), pp. 48-63, see p. 49.

8. John Dewey, "The Principle of Nationality," originally published in the *Menorah Journal,* reprinted in Dewey, *The Middle Works,* 10:285-291, see p. 289.

9. Ibid., p. 288.

10. Ibid.

11. James, *Pluralistic Universe,* pp. 321-22.

12. See, Michael Walzer et al., *The Politics of Ethnicity* (Cambridge: Harvard University Press, 1982), p. vi.

13. John Dewey, "Nationalizing Education," originally published in *Journal of Education* 84, pp. 425-28. Reprinted in Dewey, *Middle Works,* 10:201-210, see p. 205.

14. *The Collected Papers of Charles Sanders Peirce,* ed. C. Hartshorne, P. Weiss, and A. Burkes, 8 vols. (Cambridge: Harvard University Press, 1931-35, 1958), vol. 6, p 169..

15. Ibid., *CP,* vol. 1, p. 171.

16. Ibid., *CP,* vol. 1, p. 172.

17. Ibid., *CP,* vol. 1, p. 173.

18. Ibid., *CP,* vol. 1, p. 174.

19. Ibid.,*CP,* vol. 6, p. 93.

20. Horace Kallen, "Democracy versus the Melting-Pot," *Nation* 100 (February 1915), pp. 18-25.

21. Horace Kallen, *Culture and Democracy in the United States* (New York: Boni and Liveright, 1924).

22. David Hollinger, "Cultural Pluralism and Multiculturalism," in *A Companion to American Thought*, ed. R. F. Wrightman, and James Kloppenberg (Oxford and Cambridge, MA: Blackwell, 1995), pp. 162-166, see p. 163.

23. Randolph Bourne, "Transnational America," originally published in *Atlantic Monthly* 118 (July 1916), pp. 86-97; Reprinted in *The American Intellectual Tradition*, ed. David A. Hollinger, and Charles Capper, vol. II, 2nd ed. (Oxford and New York: Oxford University Press, 1993), pp. 179-188.

24. Horace Kallen et al., *Cultural Pluralism and the American Idea* (Philadelphia: University of Pennsylvania Press, 1956), p. 98.

25. Cf. John Dewey, "I Believe" originally published in *I Believe: The Personal Perspectives of Certain Eminent Men and Women of Our Time*, ed. Clifton Fadimen (New York: Simon and Schuster, 1939), pp. 347-54. Reprinted in John Dewey, *The Later Works*, ed. Jo Ann Boydston, 17 vols., (Carbondale: Southern Illinois University Press, 1981-1991), vol. 14, pp. 91-97, see, pp. 91-92; and Kallen, *Cultural Pluralism*, p. 178.

26. Cf. Leonard Harris, *The Philosophy of Alain Locke: Harlem Renaissance and Beyond* (Philadelphia: Temple University Press. 1989), pp. 6-7.

27. Alain Locke, in Harris, *Philosophy of Alain Locke*, p. 191-92).

28. Ibid., p. 213.

29. Nancy Fraser, "Another Pragmatism: Alain Locke, Critical 'Race' Theory, and the Politics of Culture," in *The Revival of Pragmatism, New Essays on Social Thought, Law, and Culture*, ed. Morris Dickstein (Durham, NC and London: Duke University Press, 1998), p. 168.

30. Ibid., p. 169.

31. Alain Locke, quoted in Charlene Haddock Seigfried, *Pragmatism and Feminism, Reweaving the Social Fabric* (Chicago: University of Chicago Press, 1996), p. 190.

32. Alain Locke, Ibid., pp. 190-191.

33. Ibid.

34. Charlene Haddock Seigfried, "Introduction," to Ralph Barton Perry, *The Thought and Character of William James* (Nashville and London: Vanderbilt University Press), pp. ix-xvii, see p. xvii.

35. Sidney Hook, *The Quest for Being* (New York: St. Martin's Press, 1961), p. 206.

36. Ibid.

37. Ibid., p. 207.

38. Ibid., p. 206.

39. Ibid., p. 207.

40. Ibid.

41. Ibid.

13

BEYOND MULTICULTURALISM
OUR RESPONSIBILITY TO HUMANITY AS A WHOLE

Paul Kurtz

I

Humanism today has special significance for the worldwide civilization that is emerging. For the first time in human history all human beings have become an integral part of a planetary community. Indeed, no part of humanity can any longer live in haughty isolation or ignorance, indifferent to the needs and interests, sufferings and achievements of other human beings. The human environment is now truly global. Whatever happens in any one corner of the world is or should be of concern to whatever happens anywhere. We can now truly realize, to paraphrase John Donne, that for whomever the bell tolls on our earthly habitat, "it tolls for thee."

Idealists of the past have long dreamt of creating a world in which genuine brotherhood and sisterhood would prevail. Suddenly this option is not mere wishful thinking, but is within the range of practicality. This is due in large measure to the impressive discoveries of science and technology, the information age, and the global economy which have enabled us to overcome the barriers of geographical separation. This has opened the possibility that every human being can relate to every other on the planet. We now have the means to significantly alter the narrow chauvinistic perspectives of the past and to enlarge our awareness of our interdependence.

Unfortunately, the world is confronted by the stark reality that nation-states still compete for power (there are now an estimated 184 countries), and that separate tribal, ethnic, religious, linguistic, and cultural enclaves still contend. If multiculturalists had their way, the world might be divided into 500 or more nation-states based upon cultural differences. But such cultural-ethnic-national divisions are often based upon ancient traditions no longer relevant, and these tend to thwart the full realization of planetary solidarity.

Historically, patterns of travel and trade, immigration and emigration have enabled people, in contiguous regions at least, to interact. The vast distances on the planet, however, were such that large sectors of the human family could develop pockets of relative economic, social, and cultural isolation. Indeed, defensive barriers against alien intrusions were erected by nations or empires which feared "barbarian invaders"—the Great Wall of China, the fortifications on the frontiers of the Roman Empire, or the Maginot and Siegfried Lines in Europe attest to this attitude. Wars of aggression and conquest were pervasive—such as Alexander's expeditionary army, the Mongol invasion of India, or the European colonial expansion throughout the world. Jingoistic appeals to nationalism and patriotism were and still are common: many nations consider that they are "chosen by God," or have "a sacred destiny" to rule, or that they are the only true paragons of Virtue and Morality.

We are confronted by two options today: First, we can encourage a multicultural world of nationalistic, cultural, ethnic, racial, and religious diversity. There is a positive aspect of multiculturalism that is noble and needs defense. We should not seek to repress cultural minorities nor be intolerant of them. This has often been the case. Thus multiculturalism has a powerful ethical claim: that we should respect cultural differences and allow them to co-exist. Tolerance is a key humanist virtue. But there can be a negative aspect to multiculturalism, for it may encourage societies to live in separation and isolation, guarding their own distinctive histories and traditions. Unfortunately this can foster mistrust and hostility—witness the tragic conflicts between Muslims and Hindus on the subcontinent, Jews and Arabs in Palestine, or the ethnic hatreds unleashed in the former Soviet Union and Yugoslavia. This separatist posture runs counter to the global civilization that is now emerging. The bloody carnages in Rwanda in Africa and East Timor in Indonesia dramatize the dangers of extreme "culturalism" run amok. I readily grant that we should appreciate and tolerate cultural diversity; but this is a far cry from allowing cultural tyranny; that is, the division of peoples by their cultural backgrounds. This form of "culturalism" can be as dangerous as "racism" or "nationalism," both of which have been responsible for wars of repression and genocide. It is a new form of Apartheid.

Interestingly, the defenders of culturalism end up in epistemological and moral anarchy. In epistemology, for example, some multiculturalists argue that "all truths are relative to the culture in which they originate." But this is contradictory, for this claim itself would be relative to the culture in which it originated; and many cultural chauvinists would reject the claim, maintaining that their cultural truth claims should be taken as gospel. How can one argue against them, if truth is relative to each culture?

Some postmodernist multiculturalists would reduce scientific theories to "social constructs," but this leads to epistemological subjectivism. If this is the case, then again multiculturalism would not be any truer than any other claim, including its contradiction, which would be absurd.

Similarly, if multiculturalism is applied to ethics there are unsettling consequences. If "good," "bad," "right," and "wrong" are relative to the culture in which they function, then on what basis can we indict cannibalism, Mayan religious sacrifice, the historic binding of female feet in China, slavery, or even Nazism. Surely there are some ethical rights and norms which we consider to be so general (or even universal); and these cut across cultural differences. Indeed, we would be prepared to defend them aside from considerations of relativity.

Still another practical objection to multiculturalism is that in many societies there is widespread intermarriage among persons of diverse racial, ethnic, and cultural backgrounds. How define such individuals—they are truly multi-racial, -cultural, and -ethnic; and in a sense transcend any effort to narrowly pigeon-hole them. We saw the tragic application of "culturalism" in Yugoslavia, where people who had lived together in peace were suddenly transformed into bitter enemies; and the sons and daughters of mixed marriages became displaced persons forced to choose between two loyalties.

This leads to a second alternative, the quest for an outlook that transcends the limits of parochial multiculturalism and attempts to find its basis in a set of moral principles rooted in world culture and civilization. this option, though respecting differences, seeks to transcend the narrow ethnic-cultural chauvinisms of the past and reaches out to create a new world civilization in which all sectors of humanity share common values. This latter option can only develop if the diverse cultures of humanity are able to integrate on some level and to live together in peace and harmony. This, I believe, is the great challenge now confronting the world; and humanism, I submit, can help us overcome ancient rivalries and create a new, more encompassing, world culture. I reiterate, this does not deny the need to preserve cherished cultural heritages and institutions, but at the same time it means that we are willing to participate in a planetary civilization that cuts across distinctive cultural lines.

Samuel P. Huntington, in his book *The Clash of Civilizations and the Remaking of the World Order*,[1] shows that the world is divided along linguistic, ethnic, religious, and cultural fault lines. Separate civilizations, he says, are now competing for the hearts and minds of men and women in their areas and throughout the world. There is rich diversity in languages. The total number of people speaking major languages in 1992 by percentages are as follows: Arabic 3.5 percent, Bengali 3.2 percent, English 7.6 percent, Hindi 6.4 percent, Mandarin 15.2 percent, Russian 4.9 percent, Spanish 6.1 percent. In China there are several languages in competition with Mandarin; these include Cantonese, Wu, Min, Hakka. European languages have extended beyond the continent and they include, besides English and Spanish, French, German, Portuguese, etc. Similarly for India and other parts of the world where there are a wide range of local dialects. Should everyone learn English, now the language of commerce, science, cultural exchange, and diplomacy? Or are there other options?

Similarly, the world can also be broken into major religious traditions. The estimated numbers of adherents are as follows: Western Christian 29.9 percent, Orthodox Christian 2.4 percent, Muslim 19.2 percent, Hindu 13.7 percent, Buddhist 5.7 percent, Chinese folk 2.5 percent, Tribal 1.6 percent, Nonreligious 17.1 percent, Atheist 4.2 percent. The question can be raised, How can humanity overcome the differences in faith systems? Humanists believe in the ethics of tolerance. Unfortunately, there is often intensive competition between the creeds. Intolerance is the result.

Humankind is also divided into nation-states. During the Cold War there were two main power blocs. Fortunately, this has broken down. There are now a pluralistic set of competing political power centers, though at the present time the United States, with vast economic, technological, and military capability, dominates the world and weakens the authority of the United Nations.

There are also racial and ethnic differences that split humankind. Prejudice and bigotry are endemic. Extreme nationalists attempt to preserve "pure" racial stocks; but this can lead to intense hatred, even genocide.

Many of these barriers to cooperation—linguistic, religious, political, racial, ethnic—developed because of the historic isolation of regions, which guarded and preserved their separate identities. Today these boundaries are blurring, and there is emerging the recognition that humankind needs to establish a more universal civilization, which would seek to transcend factional differences. This would allow independent cultural traditions to co-exist, but it would seek to find at the same time some basis for shared values and a common identity for all human beings living on the planet.

Is this desire for a universal world civilization simply a predilection of Western European civilization, given its emphasis on rationality, science, pragmatism, secularism, and democracy? Or does it have widespread appeal for the diverse cultures on the planet? I would argue that it is in the interest of all sections of humankind to help forge a more universal planetary conception of humanity.

II

Permit me to briefly review the new technological realities that now make possible this new planetary consciousness.

•There is now the actuality of instant communication by means of satellites. Internet, television, cell phones, radio, etc. make it possible for people to know what is happening every-where—whether riots in the streets of Indonesia, the trial of General Augusto Pinochet in Britain, the impeachment trial of Clinton in America, or nuclear testing in India and Pakistan. Incidentally, it is now technologically feasible to translate languages on the World Wide Web so that any language, in principle, can be understood by those who cannot speak it. English perhaps no longer need dominate the world of commerce, culture, and diplomacy.

•Rapid jet travel is a reality anywhere on the planet. By opening up and facilitating the direct exchange between peoples, an appreciation of the diverse cultural traditions and the need for negotiation and compromise is enhanced.

•Virtually all national and regional economic units are now dependent upon the global market. Global financial institutions and conglomerates govern the flow of currency and capital across frontiers and compete for world market share. Huge transnational conglomerates often have more wealth and power than independent countries, and they resist regulation on the national level. Given this reality, labor has to compete on the international scale, threatened by the effect of global conglomerates on wages and prices, and always open to the fear of downsizing and unemployment.

•Immigration and emigration continue throughout the world; as does intermarriage between diverse ethnic and racial stocks. For example, on the street in which I live in Amherst, New York, there are several Indian and Korean families who have settled in the United States only within the past 20 years. While they have prospered, their children have intermarried with children of other ethnic backgrounds. The same thing is true in Australia, Canada, Latin America, Europe, and other regions of the world.

•The standards of living and nutrition for significant sectors of the world population have improved, largely because of science and technology. This cuts across frontiers. Similarly, the medical revolution has made it possible to cure diseases, relieve suffering and pain, and extend life spans. Some infectious diseases such as influenza and AIDS are international and require cooperative preventative therapies.

•It is now possible by means of biogenetic engineering to reproduce human beings artificially and thus to redirect the course of future evolution.

•The universal right of every child on the planet to educational enrichment is now widely recognized. Knowledge of *world* history thus becomes available to everyone. This enables people to transcend narrow insularity and to widen the understanding of our interdependence.

•The arts, culinary tastes, and fashions from all corners of the globe are now available for people of diverse cultures. We can enjoy Chinese and Indian cuisine, French, Chilean, and Italian wines, Western and Oriental music, literature, poetry, drama, cinema and TV.

•The language of science and mathematics has become universal. Its theories and applications are comprehended by educated men and women no matter what their country of origin. In this context the scientific view of the cosmos competes with the ancient systems of religious metaphysics. The scientific outlook has enlarged our understanding of nature and led to a new appreciation of scientific methods of inquiry and critical thinking. Viewing the planet earth from outer space as a blue-green dot enhances our awareness of our common planetary habitat.

All of the above factors are rapidly transforming the character of the human condition. The basic question for humanists is whether humankind has reached a level in its development that enables it to reach a new global ethical consciousness. This is already occurring largely under the influence of democratic humanism. First, a set of universal human rights have been declared, which guarantees equal liberty and justice for all individuals in the world. Any violation of human rights can be instantly known and opposed, such as the repression of Andreí Sakharov or the *fatwas* against Salman Rushdie and Taslima Nasrin. Dictatorial regimes are not able to commit evil with impunity, without being called to account by the conscience of the world community. It is no longer possible for any one nation or culture to claim immunity from the Universal Declaration of Human Rights or to deny their applicability to all of their inhabitants. There is also an awareness that humans share a set of common human values—in spite of our cultural diversity. Living in the same world, facing similar problems, and having common needs, the humanist movement needs to define and defend our shared values.

III

Humanists have pointed to the need to embark upon a number of practical measures on the international level. At the International Humanist and Ethical Union Congress held in 1988 in Amherst, New York, *A Declaration of Interdependence: A New Global Ethic* was issued.[2] That *Declaration* held that there was a need to develop a new global ethical consciousness. This was again reiterated in *Humanist Manifesto 2000: A Call for a New Planetary Bill of*

Rights and Responsibilities, issued in 1999,[3] and endorsed by humanists worldwide.

I wish to focus, in the balance of this paper, on certain principles implicit in this new planetary ethics. No doubt each person has a multiple set of responsibilities relative to his or her social context: parents have obligations to their children, to bring them up, to preserve and protect them, to educate and nourish them; and this should be reciprocal, for children have duties to their parents later in life; similarly, husbands, wives or partners in a relationship or a household have obligations to each other. Individuals likewise have responsibilities to their friends, colleagues, and neighbors, and to other members within their local communities. A person has responsibilities to the extended family, the tribe, village, city, or state in which he resides. Similarly, each person has obligations within their own countries, to the laws and institutions which govern their behavior; and this is true of Indians and Englishmen, Norwegians and Chinese, Africans and Americans. We need, however, to add to these responsibilities a new responsibility that has emerged, and that is our responsibility to humanity as a whole.

Let me begin by stating several principles of ethical responsibility. Given the limited space at my disposal, I can only state them without a full justification.[4]

- The first principle is that *a rational person ought to express some moral caring about the needs of others.* We have a general obligation to be a caring person, that is, to be compassionate, empathetic, and altruistic.

- We may state another principle that follows from this: namely, where it is within our power, *we ought to mitigate the suffering, distress, pain, and sorrow of other human beings.* This principle seeks to reduce suffering where it is possible to do so. This applies to our friends, relatives, and neighbors within our communities, or other citizens in the state in which we reside. We may not always have the means or power to apply the principle to those outside of our immediate network. Within the community, where we are personally involved, I would suggest that it is incumbent upon us to do so.

•Another aspect of the principle of moral caring is positive; namely that *we ought to develop a benevolent attitude towards all persons*. Not everyone is deserving of our benevolence, those who behave indecently may be undeserving. We cannot always confer goods and benefits to others, and again we may lack the means to do so. Nonetheless, this principle lays down a general *prima facie* obligation. How it applies depends upon the concrete context. Charity begins at home, many will say, but I respond that we also should extend, where we can and if it is within our range, some positive moral caring toward all persons.

•In summary, this rule of ethical responsibility states that we ought to act so as to mitigate human suffering and sorrow and to increase the sum of human good and happiness, providing it is possible to do so. I think that the above principle applies to all civilized communities: it is recognized by both religious believers and nonbelievers. It is essential to the entire framework of human morality. No community can long endure if it violates the common moral decencies. The key question today concerns the range of these elementary principles. I submit that our moral duty should be generalized and extended to humanity as a whole. This means that we should be concerned, not only with the well-being of those within our community or nation-state, but also with the entire world community.

•Extreme chauvinistic cultural partiality is divisive. Although our loyalty to the norms of our country or ethnic group takes us beyond selfish parochial interests to a wider concern for the good of the inhabitants of the region in which we happen to live, extreme chauvinism between ethnic groups and nation-states can be destructive. Moral caring thus should not end at our ethnic enclave or national frontier. Ethical rationality enjoins us to build institutions of cooperation and to attempt, wherever possible, to negotiate our differences peacefully. The broader injunction is that *an impartial ethical rationality should apply to all human beings who have equal dignity and value.* This implies that all human beings should be treated humanely and that we should be concerned with the defense of human rights everywhere.

Accordingly, we each have a duty to help mitigate the suffering of people anywhere in the world and to contribute to the common good, thus finding some common ground with all humans. This expresses our highest sense of compassion and benevolence. This implies that people living in the affluent nations have an obligation to mitigate suffering and enhance the well-being, where they can, of people in the impoverished regions of the world, and that those in the underdeveloped areas likewise have an obligation to replace resentment against the affluent with reciprocal goodwill and to endeavor, as far as they can, to pull themselves up by their bootstraps. People should not be led to live on the dole permanently. The best we can do for them is to help them to learn how to help themselves.

IV

The full implications of these ethical injunctions is not only that they apply to humanity as a whole in the present, but that we should develop some concern about the future of humankind. We can raise the question, "What responsibilities do we have toward the future of humankind?" I think we have an overriding obligation to future posterity and that the same moral obligations to care for humanity as a whole in one's present social context also applies to the future of humanity—surely in the immediate future, but also on a long-range scale.

We may ask, What is our obligation to a future world now unseen and to generations still unborn? What do we owe to them? I submit that the same moral obligation to care for humanity as a whole in the present also applies to the future of humankind. There is, as it were, an intergenerational responsibility, a continuity across generations. Rational persons thus recognize their obligations to our common children's children's children. This means that we have an extended obligation to the community of all human beings, present and future.

•Thus,   another general principle of responsibility presents itself to us: We ought to care for the future of the human species, including future generations still unborn, and the planetary environment which they will inherit. This principle grows out of and is related to the principles of moral caring, including compassion and benevolence. We can imaginatively identify with future generations and, all things begin equal, we ought to wish them well; surely we should not seek to harm them purposely. Although as rationally prudent persons we focus on present needs and interests and those of the immediate future, we nonetheless should have some concern for future generations. We should not be impervious to the effect that our actions may have on the environment of future generations.

It may be asked, How can we be said to have an obligation to nameless and faceless persons of the future? How can they be said to have rights against us, if they do not yet exist? My response is that a right is a claim made by a person against another person or institution. If that person is yet to be born, then the right exists as a potential right in recognition of the likelihood that such a claim in the future may be made. Thus we can make a case that those still to be born have implicit rights and claims against us.

We can look back and retrospectively evaluate the actions of our forebears, and we can praise or blame them for their acts of omission or commission. We can criticize, for example, those who cut down the rain forests in Brazil or misused oil resources. Conversely, we can thank the architects and engineers of the past for the fine water-treatment plants, underground disposal systems, highways and bridges that they built and which we use today. Thus we can empathize with the future world and imaginatively project what those who will live then will be like, and we can infer obligations today for those tomorrow. Our obligation to the future stems in part from our gratitude and appreciation, or perhaps condemnation, of generations previous to ours and the sacrifices that they made from which we benefit. Future spokespersons need spokespersons today, serving as their proxies and defending their future implicit potential rights. Therefore, it can be argued that we do indeed have some obligations to the future.

- •At the very least, a general ethical principle emerges: Do nothing that would endanger the very survival of future generations of the human species and of their habitat.

- •And another principle follows from this: We should use what we need rationally and avoid wasting nonrenewable resources. To so argue is not to impose an impossible obligation, because a good portion of the human race already is morally concerned about future prosperity, including an environmental concern. We should thank our forebears who sacrificed themselves in battles against oppression or who fought revolutions to preserve liberty and justice. One might argue that it was for their own generation, but I would say it was also for posterity.

Countless men and women have struggled to ensure a more peaceful, healthful, and democratic world; they have attempted to build better institutions so that their fellow human beings could prosper. One may even argue that the heroic idealism devoted toward a beloved cause beyond themselves and for the greater good of humanity has always inspired human beings. Thus, a viable humanistic ideal focusing on a better world can engender ethical commitment, and this commitment should apply to all people, whether religious or nonreligious, theists or humanists.

The defense of these ethical principles should be high on the agenda of the world humanist movement. We need to convince our fellow human beings about the imperative that we work together in creating a new planetary humanism in which preserving humanity as a whole is our supreme obligation. What more noble mission for us to embark upon as we enter a new millennium.

Notes

1. Samuel P. Huntington, *The Clash of Civilizations and the Remaking of the World Order* (New York: Simon and Schuster, 1996).

2. See Paul Kurtz, Levi Fragell, and Rob Tielman, *Building a World Community: Humanism in the 21st Century* (Amherst, N.Y.: Prometheus Books, 1989).

3. *Humanist Manifesto 2000: A Call for a New Planetary Bill of Rights and Responsibilities*, drafted by Paul Kurtz (Amherst, N.Y.: Prometheus Books, 2000).

4. For a fuller elaboration of my thesis, see my books *The Courage to Become: The Virtues of Humanism* (Westport, Connecticut: Praeger/Greenwood, 1997) and *Forbidden Fruit: The Ethics of Humanism* (Amherst, N.Y.: Prometheus Books, 1988).

CONTRIBUTORS

Khoren Arisian
Minister Emeritus, First Unitarian Society of Minneapolis; President, Friends of Religious Humanism

Vern L. Bullough
Distinguished Professor and Dean of Natural and Social Sciences Emeritus, SUNY, Buffalo; Visiting Professor, University of Southern California

Howard G. Callaway
Adjunct Associate Professor of Philosophy, Rider University, Lawrenceville, New Jersey; Research Scholar, Seminar for Philosophy, University of Mainz, Germany

Paul Kurtz
Professor Emeritus of Philosophy, SUNY, Buffalo; Chairman, Center for Inquiry; Editor-in-Chief, *Free Inquiry* magazine

Sarah W. Oelberg
Minister, Unitarian Universalist churches in Mankato and Hanska, Minnesota

Don Page
Electrical engineer, academic, farmer, and political activist; former editor of U.S., Canadian, and international humanist magazines

Howard Radest
Former Director, Ethical Culture Schools; Leader, American Ethical Union

Philip J. Regal
Professor of Ecology, Evolution, and Behavior, University of Minnesota

Andreas Rosenberg
Professor of Laboratory Medicine, Pathology, Biochemistry, Biophysics, University of Minnesota

Harvey Sarles
Professor of Cultural Studies and Comparative Literature, University of Minnesota

Robert B. Tapp
Professor Emeritus of Humanities, Religious Studies, South Asian Studies, University of Minnesota; Dean, The Humanist Institute

Michael Werner
Businessman; former President, American Humanist Association

Carol Wintermute
Former Religious Education Director, First Unitarian Society of Minneapolis; President, North American Committee for Humanism